Praise for *The Innovation Book*

'Innovation is often seen as something others do. But, as Mckeown argues, it's something we can all do. He describes a very human, holistic approach to collective creativity complementary to Jugaad, the art of overcoming harsh conditions through frugal and flexible innovation.'

Jaideep Prabhu, Jawaharlal Nehru Professor of Indian Business and Enterprise at Judge Business School and co-author of *Jugaad Innovation*

'Written with real elegance, it oozes a presence of solid experience. I tend to require visuals but his words intrigue and enchant. It's very deep, extremely well thought out and offers a lovely pulse between framing challenges, offering insight, and suggestions to "go try this." I love that.'

Marc McLaughlin, Partner, Business Models Inc.

'Mckeown gives powerful ways of tapping your deepest wells of creativity for truly spectacular results. A remarkably accessible read, it will transform how you think, work, speak, problem-solve, and perform!'

Marshall Goldsmith, author of New York Times and global bestseller, *What Got You Here Won't Get You There*

'If I weren't so damn busy following the principles in Max's book, I would be reading it. He's an amazing presenter and communicator and has a fantastic perspective that he shares unlike anyone else I've ever met. The next best thing to seeing him live is to get inside this book.'

Clark Scheffy, Managing Director, IDEO, Global Design Consultancy

'When asked to innovate, my stomach churns, head reels and I go into a cold sweat. His opening lines quickly put these fears to rest, as Max describes innovation as "practical creativity" – making new ideas useful.' And, with his book in hand, that's something I can confidently do.'
Scott Smith, Head of Business Development, Microsoft MDS

'This is an amazing book! Combining a solid command of the relevant concepts with a thorough appreciation of practical relevance, it provides a comprehensive source for scholars and real world innovators alike.'
Claus D. Jacobs, Professor of Strategy, Berne Polytechnic School of Management; Associate Fellow, Oxford; co-author of *Crafting Strategy*

'Max is like the Innovation Chef equivalent of Gordon Ramsey. Whether or not you invite Max to help with boosting innovation, it is certain that his cookbook will very quickly earn its dog-eared corners from daily use.'
Dr Adrian S. Petrescu, Professor, College of Business, Bellevue University, Nebraska; President and CEO of InnovationTrek

'People often ask: "What is innovation?" and "How can we do more?" For curious and brave disrupters, it's a guide to ensure good ideas succeed!'
Aimie Smith Chapple, Innovation Lead for Accenture UKI

'Max always inspires me with astonishingly wise thoughts that are strategic, inspiring and easy to follow. That's what makes this book so powerful, it gives you the belief that innovation is within your ability.'
Kevin Spreekmeester, Senior VP Marketing, Canada Goose Inc

'The great joy is how it helps you make sense of innovation. Whether you want to nurture your own ideas – or help colleagues – it's all here!'
Bernie Ritchie, Independent Marketing Consultant, @ managementsushi

'Mckeown shares my view, based on long experience, that innovation is a verb. It's about doing. The challenge is how to shape the climate to let ideas spring up, grow and mature! A book to be read and read again.'
Shaun Coffey, Science and Business Entrepreneur and Chief Executive

'Steve Jobs talked about man as tool maker: innovation is like that, it's about making new things useful, and can make the difference between life and death, evolution and extinction. This book is like a bible for us.'
Diego Caravana, co-founder and CTO, Crowd Emotion Ltd

'All about seeing and doing things differently – not just talking about it. For all those who aspire to be innovative. It distils decades of evidence and theory. Spoiler: might replace your need for mediocre outside help!'
Prescott C. Ensign, Dobson Professor of Innovation and Entrepreneurship, Wilfrid Laurier University, Canada

'Highly recommended. A structured, practical book for innovators in every sphere – business, social innovation, social enterprises, government, not-for-profits, arts and education.'
Suhit Anantula, Director, The Australian Centre for Social Innovation

'An important reminder that innovation is about useful ideas that *do good*. With shrewd advice and models from scientists, economists and psychologists, there's something here for everyone.'
Lucy Gower, Innovation Director, Clayton Burnett

'Mckeown combines an encyclopaedic toolkit for innovators with a depth of practical experience. His explanations stimulate many reflections on Innovation and prompt creative actions to follow through with.'
Grier Palmer, Creativity Director, Warwick Business School

'To successfully condense this huge topic is a big ask but it certainly delivers. It's clear that Max has discussed, debated and challenged each section, tool and topic to ensure every page earns its keep.'
Matt Stocker, Director, Stocker Partnership

'A master class for understanding innovation. A practical and methodically delivered guide, clearly explained with a passion for the subject, this book does exactly what it says on the tin!'
Ruby S. Azzopardi, Innovation Consultant, Cranfield Trust

'A most compelling and complete description of true innovation. You will see yourself in this book, especially if you are passionately curious and, perhaps a bit "different"...'
Kim Schmidt, Program Manager, D&B MVP Program, Medical Automation Research Center as Google GLASS and Medical Expert

'This book is a must-read. It connects the larger body of innovative thought with pragmatic real world issues. And treats important issues – especially uncomfortable ones – with refreshing directness.'
Greg Stewart, Innovator, Senior Fellow, Honeywell

'Mckeown successfully synthesises an enormous amount of knowledge. Max knows what he writes, and writes what he knows. It's honest and thorough without pretending innovation is simplistic. Compelling.'
Professor Alf Rehn, innovation critic, thought-leader and author of *Dangerous Ideas*

'This book presents a comprehensive and easy-to-use toolkit for strategic innovation. It goes a long way to empowering innovators and innovation managers alike.'
Vinay Dabholkar, Professor, Institute of Product Leadership and author of *8 Steps to Innovation*

'This is an excellent and unique work on innovation. Mckeown offers actionable advice, and a comprehensive overview of the discipline's rich body of knowledge. Perfect executive education material!'

Dr John Gøtze, Editor-in-Chief, QualiWare Center of Excellence, co-author of *Beyond Alignment*

'As a student, I always wished there was one book that brought the different theories and examples together. Highly recommended to high achievers and adventurers plunging into real-world innovation.'

Olivia Yunji Cho, graduate student on MA in Innovation Management, Central St Martins College of Arts and Design

'Among its outstanding strengths, the most remarkable is a belief in human capabilities and potential. The author contextualises his ideas in the history of humankind and shows how innovators can succeed.'

Dr Beatriz Junquera, Professor of Management and Innovation, University de Oviedo

'Where this goes beyond is organising ideas into powerful learning modules with in-depth analysis and know-how. Readers will be rewarded with new expertise from this comprehensive exploration of innovation.'

Paul R. Williams, PMP, Vice President, Operations and Technology and Lead at Associated Bank, delivering innovation through project management

'An advocate for effective creative thinking and successfully surfing waves of change, Mckeown encourages everyone to raise their Innovation Quotient (InQ). This book is of great importance to us all.'

Kim Chandler McDonald, Strategic Innovation Consultant and author of *Innovation: how innovators think, act, and change our world*

'Innovation is a tough game; that's why it's worth reading Max's book for stimulus, advice, and direction. Sound guidance, fluidly and enjoyably written, a book to read, keep close by and refer to regularly.'

Kevin McFarthing, founder of Innovation Fixer, open innovation expert, ex-director, R&D Reckitt Benckhiser

'For the veteran, valuable insights to keep your leadership practices fresh and vibrant. For the novice, clear "how to" approaches to develop your innovation knowledge and competence to become a veteran innovator.'

Kwaku Atuahene-Gima, Professor of Marketing and Innovation Management, China Europe International Business School

'A truly fabulous example of Mckeown's ability to translate core theories into real life. It will travel with me on my innovation quest. Another masterpiece that will be used and suitable for the many.'

Dr Sanjeev Gogna, Head of Innovation, Celesio UK and visiting lecturer (Innovation and Creativity Module) Warwick Business School

'Like your own personal innovation coach, nudging you with insights, tips and tricks. From ideation to company politics to realisation, Max will re-motivate when spirits are low, and give you wings when energy is high.'

Kosta Peric, Deputy Director, Financial Services for the Poor at Bill & Melinda Gates Foundation and author of *The Castle and The Sandbox*

'It is a challenge for me to see myself as very creative, so I appreciate the book's tangible, helpful tools, examples and approaches that bring practicality and creativity together to generate meaningful innovation.'

Greg Richardson, The Strategic Monk

'Read it with a notepad nearby so you do not miss the ideas, action items, and insights that will continually challenge your thinking and change your current direction. Provocative and essential.'

Skip Prichard, President and CEO, OCLC

'Mckeown has created a very readable and practical book which allows the reader to quickly grasp key elements and enable them to perhaps start their own journey of exploration!'
Tejal Fatania, Associate Director, Ernst & Young, change and transformation specialist

'*The Innovation Book* turns creative rebels into innovation magicians, with plenty of hands-on practical examples and tips. A great resource for change agents who want to change the world.'
Helene Finidori, Consultant in Transformative Action, Professor of Management and Leadership of Change, Staffordshire University

'Great innovation has depth, and Mckeown's book has impressive depth. It explores how to be creative, make new ideas useful – all in easily explainable language. Great book. Wish I'd read it years ago.'
Herbert Roberts, Innovationologist at GE Aviation

'One of the most useful handbooks I've read as it guides through theory and practical steps. But more than this, it's written with both wisdom and wit. Essential reading and a highly prized addition to my library.'
Roger Bromley, Visiting Professor of Innovation and Collaboration, University of Huddersfield

'I enjoyed it! Clearly written without losing the intelligence of the ideas. Connects an impressive range of concepts with up-to-date examples and a focus on the creative self that is often overlooked.'
Professor Fiona Lettice, Professor of Innovation Management, Norwich Business School and Visiting Research Fellow at Cranfield University

'Full of valuable insights – Mckeown's book is both challenging and supportive. A handbook to be used continually as an aid to innovation.'
Professor David Crowther, De Montfort University Business School and Editor, *Social Responsibility Journal*

'Loved the book! Great examples, easy read and valuable tools!'
Jay Rao, Professor of Innovation and Strategy, Babson College, Boston, No 1 in MBA for Entrepreneurship for 20 years

'Compulsory reading for each entrepreneur, innovator and CEO. In a world where others disrupt your business model, you need continuous innovation. Max guides us skilfully through the jungle of approaches.'
Tilmann Laurence Gabriel, business model innovation expert and serial entrepreneur, Munich, Germany

'It's excellent. A real authority. An easy-to-read, comprehensive, and insightful guide. A book I will buy myself and recommend to others.'
Clive Harris, Innovation Consultant and IBM Distinguished Engineer

'A complete manual for innovation practitioners. Deeply conceptualised and perfectly sequenced. An outstanding reference for managing ideas.'
Xavier Ferras, MBA, PhD, Dean, Faculty of Business and Communication. University of Vic, Visiting Professor, ESADE Business School

'The book is a treasure that re-energizes brain muscles for experts and beginners. His wise words help you get started and keep going.'
Vivian Berni, Senior Adviser at DHL

'Very valuable. The uniqueness is the dipping in/out possibilities. That's what I do with *The Strategy Book* and Mckeown has made it easy to do the same with innovation. Brilliant!'
Roy Sandbach, Professor of Innovation, Newcastle University Business School, Former Research Fellow, Proctor & Gamble

'Mckeown seamlessly merges theory with daily practice: with sparkling insights and practical tips for anyone passionate about new ideas.'
Guido Kerkhof, Marketing Consultant, Innovator at 2ignite. nl

'This is a profoundly practical book that reflects the light hand of a true master. Mckeown is just plain good at explaining things.'
Dr Kate Hammer, commercial storyteller and start-up veteran co-founder of KILN inventors of IdeaKeg, creator of StoryFORMs

'The road to successful innovation is paved with trials, mistakes and pitfalls. *The Innovation Book* delivers an essential guide for this journey.'
Professor Darren Dalcher, Director, National Centre for Project Management and Editor-in-Chief, *Journal of Software: Evolution and Process*

'Anyone wanting an adaptable and innovative organisation can do no better than read this fascinating book.'
Linda Holbeche PhD, co-author of *Engaged: unleashing the potential of your organization through employee engagement*

'A true leader needs to be a generator and stimulator for change through innovative ideas. This book is an imperative companion on your way up.'
Ludo Vandervelden, Solvay Fellow at Vrije Universiteit Brussel, Director Arcadia Strategoi, previously VP, Toyota Motor Europe

'Innovation is challenging for leaders juggling priorities. Max's unique ability is to instil innovation into *how* we do business on a daily basis.'
Paul Walters, General Manager, The Langham London

'Two words for this book: AWE-SOME.'
Raúl Lagomarsino Dutra, Professor of Innovation, ESE Business School, Santiago, Chile

'It's both a tool box *and* a rule book.'
Ellen DiResta, experience designer and innovator, Becton Dickinson

'Everyone needs to be creative in the 21st century. Dr Max clearly shows us how to boost your creative skills to become an innovator.'
Ryuta Kono, Visiting Professor at TAMA Graduate School of Business

The Innovation Book

The Innovation Book

How to manage ideas and execution for outstanding results

Max Mckeown

Harlow, England • London • New York • Boston • San Francisco • Toronto • Sydney
Auckland • Singapore • Hong Kong • Tokyo • Seoul • Taipei • New Delhi
Cape Town • São Paulo • Mexico City • Madrid • Amsterdam • Munich • Paris • Milan

PEARSON EDUCATION LIMITED

Edinburgh Gate
Harlow CM20 2JE
United Kingdom
Tel: +44 (0)1279 623623
Web: www.pearson.com/uk

First published 2014 (print and electronic)

© Maverick & Strong Limited 2014 (print and electronic)

The right of Max Mckeown to be identified as author of this work has been asserted
by him in accordance with the Copyright, Designs and Patents Act 1988.

Pearson Education is not responsible for the content of third-party internet sites.

ISBN: 978-1-292-01190-5 (print)
        978-1-292-01192-9 (PDF)
        978-1-292-01193-6 (ePub)
        978-1-292-01191-2 (eText)

British Library Cataloguing-in-Publication Data
A catalogue record for the print edition is available from the British Library

Library of Congress Cataloging-in-Publication Data
Mckeown, Max.
  The innovation book: how to manage ideas and execution for outstanding results /
Max Mckeown.
     pages cm
  Includes index.
  ISBN 978-1-292-01190-5 (pbk.)
  1. Creative ability in business. 2. Creative thinking. 3. Strategic planning. 4. New
products. 5. Diffusion of innovations--Management. 6. Technological innovations--
Management. I. Title.
  HD53.M386 2014
  658.4'063--dc23
                                    2014015485

10 9 8 7 6 5 4 3 2 1
18 17 16 15 14

Cover design: David Carroll & Co.

Typeset in 9pt Stone Serif by 3
Printed in Great Britain by Henry Ling Ltd., at the Dorset Press, Dorchester

NOTE THAT ANY PAGE CROSS REFERENCES REFER TO THE PRINT EDITION

Contents

About the author

Dr. Max Mckeown is a consultant and public speaker on strategic innovation – and best-selling author of the award winning *The Strategy Book*, *Adaptability*, and several other books which have been translated into ten different languages.

Max is a Fellow of the Royal Society for the encouragement of Arts, Manufacturers and Commerce, a member of the British Psychological Society and has both an MBA and PhD from Warwick Business School where he conducts research into strategic thinking, cognition and innovation leadership.

He is also a French-speaking, London-born, Arsenal-supporting, night-clubbing fan of creative rebels.

Find more material about his work at www.maxmckeown.com

Join the conversation about shaping a better future by following him on Twitter @maxmckeown

Author's acknowledgements

'We are willing to invent.
We are willing to think long-term.
And very importantly, we are willing to be
misunderstood for long periods of time...'
Jeff Bezos, founder of Amazon

It's been my pleasure – and pain – to work with thousands of rebels, mavericks, dissenters and dreamers. Thanks to those people who've worked together to make innovation and strategy work. Comparing innovation theory with real-world innovation is at the heart of *The Innovation Book*.

Particular thanks go to those who have been part of the creative conversations throughout a very iterative writing process – and to those who have debated strategy and innovation ideas with me. They have prodded the theories, provoked improvements, and encouraged efforts to make the ideas as useful, and usable, as possible without losing their insights, depth and practical power.

Reviewers and supporters included Broc Edwards, Ralph Steiner, Greg Richardson, Cesar Malacon, Hutch Carpenter, Vivian Berni, Ron Donaldson, Alexander Brem, James Canton, John Vary, Bonnie Koenig, Jason Jaswani, Jon Pincus, Ian Taylor, Fabian Tilmant, Jeff Marsden, Fiona Lettice, Roger Bromley, Kwaku Atuahene-Gima, Irene Buchine, Richard Platt, Herb Roberts, Conor Neill, Rob Sheffield, Alf Rehn, Kate Hammer, Guido Kerkhof, Bjorn Wigforss, Allan M. Jordan, Dilip Mutum, Genco Ilgin Elcora, Saul Kaplan, Tony Morgan, Nathanael Boehm, Ben Sington, Soren Kaplan, Sandy Maxey, Claire Calmejane, Mike Brown, Jean Baptise Mac Luckie. There have been many others

– especially those in my twitter stream @maxmckeown who continue to bring me insight and valuable questions for real world innovation.

Thanks also go to my publishing team. To Nicole Eggleton, commissioning editor, who demonstrated rare understanding of how valuable each little change, and radical restructure, would be to readers and innovators. And to Laura Blake and Lucy Carter whose patient enthusiasm guided the corrections, permissions and revisions to ensure the quality of this book.

And to the thinkers and makers, past and present, who inspired this book and continue to shape the future in wonderful, unlikely, absurd, beautiful ways.

Publisher's acknowledgements

We are grateful to the following for permission to reproduce copyright material:

Figures

Figure on p.154 from Burgelman, R.A. and Siegel, R.E. 'Defining the minimum winning game in high-technology venture,' in *California Management Review*, © 2007 by the Regents of the University of California. Published by the University of California Press; Figure on page 158 from 'What is creative problem solving?', www.creativeeducationfoundation.org/our-process/what-is-cps, Creative Education Foundation; Figure on page 165 from *Business Model Generation: A Handbook for Visionaries, Game Changers, and Challengers*, Osterwalder, A. and Pigneur, Y. © 2010. Reproduced with permission of John Wiley & Sons Ltd.; Figure on page 168 from Amabile, T.M., 'Motivating creativity in organizations: on doing what you love and loving what you do,' in *California Management Review*, © 1997 by the Regents of the University of California. Published by the University of California Press; Figure on page 182 from *The innovators solution: Creating and sustaining successful growth*. Harvard Business Press (Christensen, C.M. and Raynor, M.E. 2003) p.44, Figure 3.1; Figure on page 185 from *The Innovation Journey*, by D.E. Polley et al (2008): Figure 2.1 (p.25) © 1999 by Oxford University Press, Inc. by permission of Oxford University Press, USA; Figure on page 189 from figures from History of Mechanical Inventions, Second Edition, 1954; by permission of estate of A.P. Usher; Figure on page 193 © 2013 Biomimicry 3.8. Licensed under Creative Commons BY-NC-ND. Challenge to Biology g3; Figure on page 197 from *The Innovation*

Journey by D.E. Polley et al (2008): Figure 4.7 (p.116) © 1999 by Oxford University Press, Inc., by permission of Oxford University Press, USA; Figure on page 201 from *Rational analysis for a problematic world*, Rosenhead, J. and Mingers, J. © 2001 John Wiley & Sons Ltd. Reproduced with permission of John Wiley & Sons Ltd.; Figure on page 204 reprinted from *Research Policy*, Vol 15/6, Teece, David, J., Profiting from technological innovation: implications for integration, collaboration, licensing and public policy, 285-305, © 1986, with permission from Elsevier; Figure on page 212 from Architectural Innovation: The Reconfiguration of Existing Product Technologies and the Failure of Established Firms, *Administrative Science Quarterly*, 35(1), 9-30 (Henderson, R.M. and Clark, K.B., 1990); Figure on page 216 adapted with the permission of Simon & Schuster Publishing Group from the Free Press edition of *Diffusion of Innovations*, 5th edition by Everett M. Rogers. Copyright © 1993, 2005 by Everett M. Rogers. Copyright © 1962, 1971, 1983 by the Free Press. All rights reserved.; Figure on page 220 from Abernathy, William, *Productivity Dilemma: Roadblock to Innovation in the Automobile Industry*. pp. 72, Figure 4.1. © 1978 by William J. Abernathy. Reprinted with permission of Johns Hopkins University Press; Figure on page 223 from *Open Innovation: Researching a New Paradigm* by H. Chesborough (2008): adapted versions (as agreed) of figures 1.1 and 1.2 (p.3) © Oxford University Press 2006, by permission of Oxford University Press; Figure on page 231 republished with permission of the Association for Supervision and Curriculum Development from Critical thinking through structured controversy, David W. Johnson and Roger T. Johnson, *Educational Leadership*, 1988; permission conveyed through Copyright Clearance Center, Inc.; Figure on page 235 adapted from *The Oxford Handbook of Innovation* edited by Jan Fagerberg et al (2006): Adapted version (as agreed) of Figure 3.3 (p.64) from chapter 'Networks of Innovators' by Walter Powell & Stine Grodal © Oxford University Press, by permission of Oxford University Press; Figure on page 239 from *The Essence of Winning and Losing*, 28 June 1995, by Boyd, J.R. © Col. John R. Boyd, estate.

QR Code is a registered trademark of DENSO WAVE INCORPORATED.

In some instances we have been unable to trace the owners of copyright material, and we would appreciate any information that would enable us to do so.

Introduction

'Innovation is serendipity. You never know what people are going to make next.'
Tim Berners-Lee

Innovation is about practical creativity, it's about making new ideas useful. You can use the knowledge in this book to become a more effective creative thinker. You can become a leader who can encourage others to make new ideas successful. If you are ambitious, you can use the powerful innovation lessons and tools in this book to *shape your future*.

The Innovation Book has its own innovations. It is straightforward without dumbing down ideas. It is simple to use yet based on a core set of intelligent foundations. It offers clear explanations of tools and approaches to innovation.

The ideas are based on hard-won experience and knowledge working with some of the world's most admired corporations and organisations. Some faced problems and crisis. Some wanted to do the impossible. Or change their world. They all wanted to bring beautiful ideas to life.

This book will help in all those situations. It will help whether you're studying innovation, as part of a course or degree, or as part of your job. You can also apply many of the ideas to your day-to-day life. Innovation is about solving problems creatively – useful wherever we want to make something better. New ideas can solve problems and create opportunities.

Learning about innovation is important but often frustrating because the wisdom and experience about innovation is not gathered together in one place. The action topics here are about giving you the best ideas about innovation all wrapped up in a usable, enjoyable package.

Take this book with you to work. Read it in the shower. Make notes. Draw diagrams. Tear out pages and pin them to your walls. Make the ideas come alive. Use it to provoke, comfort and inspire.

'Creativity requires courage.'
Henri Matisse

 As an experiment, this QR code can be used to access a welcome message from the author. Just download any free QR scanner app onto your smartphone or tablet from your app store. Then scan the code by pointing the camera of your device towards the code. It will read the code and take you to the web page linked to the code.

How to use this book

The Innovation Book is organised into six parts. The first four parts tackle the really important challenges that an innovator or team of any size will face in creating new ideas and moving from new ideas to successful innovation. Each part is sub-divided into specific action topics. You can dip in and out of each topic as you choose. They have been written clearly so that you can benefit from the experience and expertise in these pages whether you are a novice or an expert.

Each of the action topics has the following structure:

- **Headline description** – introduces the topic with a brief summary to get your creative juices flowing. This section suggests how often the challenge will be relevant, who on your team should be involved and the relative importance of particular action topics with a five-star rating system. The six most vital action topics are designated the innovation6.

- **Innovation examples** – so you can read about others that faced the innovation challenge and use the principles to solve problems with new ideas. This is a powerful way to learn.

- **Objective** – explains why the subject matters and what you should be trying to achieve. It also provides key concepts and explanations.

- **Context** – how the subject fits into the broader pattern of innovation and real-world situations.

- **Challenge** – why the subject is difficult and valuable. And points out ways of succeeding with the challenge effectively as an innovator.

- **Success** – describes what must happen to succeed with the innovation challenge.
- **Innovator's measure of success** – how you can assess your own progress.
- **Innovator's checklist** – a summary of actions to put the innovation principle into action.
- **Related ideas** – a suggestion of ideas from other writers – or other research – that supports or complements the innovation topic.
- **One more thing** – some inspiration to help you to make innovation succeed.
- **Do this now!** – Simple actions you can take *now* to bring new ideas to life. Start small, think big.

The fifth part is the **Innovator's turning points**. Each case explores a distinct part of the innovation-adaptation journey in more detail. Starting with recognising you have a problem, then understanding what you need to do to adapt, or innovate, and finally doing what is necessary to successfully adapt.

The sixth part is the **Innovator's toolkit**. The most important models and tools of innovation are explained in very precise, practical and efficient terms. This is intentional so that you can focus on learning, remembering and using them to achieve your real-world objectives and dreams. They include **insights for innovators** along with **related ideas** and examples of **innovation in action**.

There are different ways of using *The Innovation Book*. You can work your way through part by part. You can also skip between parts. Move between specific action topics back to the tools that best help your innovation thinking and action. Read it several times. Make notes of links between topics and tools that you find. With innovation everything is connected to everything else. The book includes cross-references to get you started. And if you add your own links it will help make innovation work for you.

The Innovation Book is clearly structured, full of practical wisdom from real-world innovators, and easy to use. It's been designed so that you will refer back to it again and again.

What is innovation?

Innovation – or practical creativity – is mainly about *making* new ideas useful. There is a lot of buzz and baggage about the word 'innovation' and this definition goes to the heart of what it is and is not. As an innovator, you can solve old problems with new ideas or you can solve new problems with old ideas used in radically different ways. As a practical creative problem-solver, it helps to understand more about how to succeed with innovation and how to make innovation succeed.

The idea of Edison as a lone creative genius isn't really true. He was creative but not alone. He was creative, but also made new ideas work by moving from idea to action. He didn't invent the light bulb but he did test light bulbs until he found a design that would be popular in the real world. He saw the future, not just in terms of science fiction but in practical industrial terms. He wasn't necessarily the best engineer but worked with a talented team inside and outside his own workshop. He had to be a creator, collaborator, entrepreneur and social climber to make the ideas work.

Objective

The history of innovation is essentially the history of practical creative problem-solving which is – pretty much – the history of what it means to be human. Our curiosity drives us to explore. Our desire drives us to improve. There are benefits to understanding how innovation is usually discussed in successful organisations and some heavyweight research. It will help you understand innovation and to see its nature, limitations and purpose. Understanding innovation will make you a more effective innovator.

Waves of creativity are unstoppable. Unfortunately, those who ignore new ideas can be stranded by progress, or smashed as they attempt to stand against the remarkable power of new ideas. Others choose to become part of the turbulent creative process, enjoying the rush of beautiful possibility and fabulous excess. Innovators choose to shape and surf waves that take us into the future.

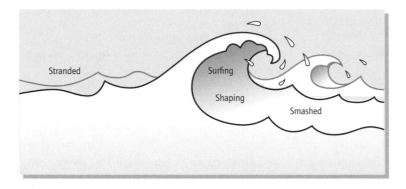

Pre-historic innovation

Around 500,000 years ago, some of our distant ancestors managed to start using fire in a, more or less, deliberate way. Later, perhaps 200,000 years ago, anatomically modern humans evolved big modern brains that gave them all sorts of advantages and led to behaviourally modern – or at least modern*ish* – people. About 50,000 years ago, we'd developed some kind of language, the ability to think in the abstract and work together. We'd also found a talent for copying ideas from each other and sharing ideas from show-how to cave painting to hieroglyphics.

Little by little, step by step, accident by accident, we learned our way towards the present day. Stones were first grasped, then used to smash, and then struck to create sharp edges that could cut or crush plants, animals or rivals. The idea for simple tool-making appears to have been discovered and used again and again by individuals as if for the first time. Later, bigger, better tools were developed and made deliberately as the tool-making idea evolved along with our creative ability.

Ancient innovation

The word 'innovation' has its origins in the Latin word *innovat* which means to renew or alter. The roots come from *in* – or into – and *novare* – or make new – which taken together suggests something being made into something else entirely new. And by the time, the Latin language was developed, some 50,000 years after the first culturally modern human, some of us had also become remarkably modern at the business of creative problem-solving and innovation.

We had invented the bow and arrow, and agriculture, domesticated animals, developed pottery and learned to weave. Some of us figured out how to irrigate crops, others how to smelt copper for tools, then bronze and iron. The ancestors of those living in Iraq, Syria, Turkey, Iran and Kuwait – or Mesopotamia – gave us the wheel, written language and glass. Those in China invented the abacus, those in Egypt the calendar while the Greeks gave us the catapult. As populations grew, so did our desire to live in larger groups. And the more of us that gathered together in one place, the more we shared. New and old ideas competed for attention. We fought, but also discovered, copied and invented.

Modern innovation

Although we'd been creatively problem-solving for thousands of years, the development of the printing press, in the 14th century, fed and nurtured a new enthusiasm for the pursuit of knowledge through discovery and learning. While not universal, this *renaissance* was deliberate, wide-spread and contagious. It developed principles for describing laws of nature – how things worked – and aimed to use that knowledge to improve human life through practical inventions and innovation.

New and old ideas continued to do battle, often with dogma and tradition. Those in power were also suspicious of the disruptive energy of ideas to change the nature of society. Some rulers sought influence through harnessing the new waves of knowledge, while others fought each new tide. Galileo was famously forced to kneel and recant his insights about the earth revolving around the sun but, despite this kind of persecution, the curious continued to connect with the curious.

By the 17th century, the west was benefiting from an increasingly methodical approach to discovering knowledge, through science, sharing what was discovered, via education and media, and making knowledge useful at the hands of inventors, workers, industry and society more generally.

Through to the 21st century, the flow of new ideas was never entirely predictable or completely painless – yet seemed unstoppable. Revolutions in agriculture, industry, medicine, transport and computing have continued in waves. Some waves are below and others above the surface, driven by the restless curiosity of creative obsessives and the near insatiable appetite for newer and better.

Context

Innovation – like strategy – started to get a lot of attention from the 1950s. Nations and corporations wanted to harness the power of new ideas for much needed growth. Leaders wanted to use those new ideas in a predictable factory of inventiveness. There was a lot of discussion about how to best *manage* a pipeline of innovation so that new products could provide an engine for economic health.

There wasn't so much discussion about how new ideas were created. There was very little debate about how to organise the best conditions *for* creativity and innovation. People focused on how to share them (diffusion) and use them (exploitation). It was only later that mainstream attention turned to how people create new insights (exploration) and ideas (generation).

Joseph Schumpeter, an economist, proposed theories about gales of creative destruction that become popular. He argued that economic growth was fuelled by new ideas that led to cycles of economic revolution. These new ideas were generated by entrepreneurs and inventors who disrupted existing business and industry to create new industries before again being disrupted.

Everett Rogers, a sociologist, described how innovations are shared and communicated in a predictable bell-curve from innovators (2.5%), early adopters (13.5%), an early majority (34%) and finally to the laggards (16%). His research began with social change in rural communities yet was eventually applied to innovations in a range of markets including – most recently – the internet (see adoption and diffusion curve on page 216).

Eric Von Hippel, an economist, argued that the majority of innovation comes from the people who need the innovation rather than R&D laboratories. He described them as *lead users* – they are the user-innovators who tinker with existing ideas or machines to find better solutions to real-world problems. These innovations may – eventually – achieve large-scale popularity or production.

Genrikh Altshuller, an engineer, created a theory of inventive problem-solving known as TRIZ. This theory was based on a set of generic rules he had discovered from researching differences between various inventions. He made a distinction between ideas that only appear to be new, ideas that are just improvements, ideas that are within the current system, ideas that improve the system and true innovation: the 0.05% of ideas that create a whole new, better, smarter system for everyone (see pages 150 and 161).

Alex Osborn, an advertising executive, developed a seven-step framework for deliberate creative problem-solving known as CPS. This framework was strongly influenced by reading of the work of psychologist George Walls on the four stages of creativity (preparation, incubation, illumination and verification). He was particularly interested in how to inspire the human imagination of individuals and groups – including his description of *brainstorming*. There are many, many similar models (see page 158).

Robert Sternberg, a psychologist, introduced some concepts that are very helpful to innovation in his three-part model of intelligence: first, *analytic intelligence*, solving well-defined problems by following predefined rules; second, *creative intelligence*, using existing knowledge and a different perspective to find new solutions; and third, *practical intelligence*, adapting yourself to a situation, and the situation to you. All three are highly relevant to the individual side of innovation.

There are other figures in innovation. There are the famous inventors, the management gurus and the academics. From Edison to Dyson, Zuckerberg to Berners-Lee, Drucker to Taylor, Deming to De Bono, Christensen to Chesbrough, Tidd and Bessant to Burns and Stalker and Amabile to Van De Ven. Ideas from all these, and many more, will feature in *The Innovation Book*. Not all of them are equally famous and some of them have worked in almost complete isolation from each other. Yet all matter.

In some ways, the intellectual history of innovation and creativity is more complex than my short introduction. Yet in other ways, it is simpler. Different people have focused on different parts of innovation. Some people focused on idea generation and how to be more creative. Some people studied idea development and how to make new ideas useful, while others examined idea diffusion, how to share and exploit the usefulness of the new idea.

Some argue for a more predictable step-by-step approach to innovation. Often because they're looking at the part of innovation that is most certain. The part where unknowns become known and tried-and-tested methods can deliver solutions based on the new idea. Others argue for an unpredictable, almost random, approach to innovation. Often because they are looking at the part of innovation that is the most uncertain – where unknowns outnumber the knowns (see page 227).

The smart innovator learns that making a new idea useful will involve different levels of certainty and uncertainty. Some stages will be random, others orderly, some episodic, while other parts will be chaotic and ambiguous. Every part of the innovation process is important, so the most successful innovators ask questions about what balance of these approaches is most relevant to any particular situation.

Challenge

Some ideas are very new, others are barely new at all. Some innovations are radical, while others are incremental. The newer an idea is, the greater the uncertainty attached to that idea. If you've got an idea that is new to the world then there is no certainty that it will ever be made to work. If you need, or want, to have an idea that is new to the world, and radically different from all other ideas, there is no guarantee you will ever find what you wanted to find. Radically new may be radically uncertain.

The smart innovator understands the trade-off between newness and control. The less that is known about an idea, the less control there is about how that idea can be found and made useful (see page 74). Sometimes the uncertainty is about having an idea that seems to solve the problem. Sometimes it's about how to make the idea happen. And at other times it will be about whether the idea actually solves a valuable problem in the real world – a mixture of functionality and popularity (see page 220).

Success

You'll know that you understand more about innovation when you see how different kinds of new ideas require, or cause, different levels of change around them. You'll recognise that different stages of innovation require different kinds of thinking and action. You'll also be able to combine the tools and principles throughout this book to think – and act – like a smart innovator.

You will learn how to create better (more useful) ideas, how new ideas become popular and how to inspire other people to innovate. You'll find insights from the psychology of creativity and collaboration to improve your ability to be a smart innovator, someone who can solve problems creatively, and be an effective part of improving the world by contributing great new ideas.

Innovator's measure of success

➤ The basic origins of modern thinking on innovation are understood.

➤ The difference between new-new innovation and new-old innovation is recognised.

➤ Tools for generating, collaborating and popularising innovation are used together.

➤ Radical and incremental innovation is treated differently.

➤ You know there is more to innovation success than a new idea or new project.

Pitfalls

It's easy to overplay order or chaos. Some of that is about your personality. You may enjoy the mess of creativity, the thrill of new ideas or the invigorating company of creative people. Alternatively, you may like to keep things neat and tidy and have a talent for efficiently organising effort. Some of this is about your experience. You may have no experience and find it difficult to navigate ambiguity and constantly changing objectives, opinions and opportunities. Or you may have lots of experience and find it too easy to prejudge the best answer to every question or rely on inflexible assumptions.

Innovator's checklist

- ▓ Consider the difference between creative destruction and incremental improvement (see page 212).

- ▓ Think about whether you (or your group) rely more on chaos or order (see page 231 for constructive controversy).

- ▓ Explore the stages of innovation and how order and chaos help or hinder (see Schroeder's innovation journey on page 185).

- ▓ Keep referring back to the basic distinction between chaos (divergence) and order (convergence) through the book so you remember to use tools in both ways (see page 172 in The innovator's toolkit).

▓ Introduce both chaotic (divergent) and order (convergent) approaches to your team. Discuss how they have been used in the past and how you could alter the balance in the future.

Related ideas

Guilford was a psychologist who made a distinction between *divergent production* and *convergent reproduction*. According to him, divergent production – fluidly creating many different ideas or many different answers to the same question – was the mark of creativity. In his view, convergent reproduction – the tendency to find just one answer to a question – was essentially uncreative. In the real world, innovation is a mixture of divergent *and* convergent thinking (and action). You need both (see page 175).

One more thing

Some 30% of cyclists don't wear a bike helmet. Some argue it ruins the spontaneity of cycling, that helmets are inconvenient, ugly and 'look silly'. Two industrial designers in Sweden saw that the product had to change (rather than the customer). Instead of more regulation they created less ugliness. They designed an invisible bike-helmet. It looks like a scarf but contains an air bag.

Clever computing recognises when the cyclist is about to crash. It ensures that a beautiful protective cocoon expands to protect the delicate bone and tissue of brain and head. In a similar way, the original idea, born while its inventors were still at university, has been nurtured and protected by a cocoon of supporting ideas. Specialists have ensured that the product passes safety regulations. Fashion brands have designed scarf covers to match your wardrobe. Vocal evangelists have been converted.

one

Your creative self

'Creativity comes from looking for the unexpected and
stepping outside of your own experience.'
Masaru Ibuka, Founder of Sony

To become a more effective innovator, start with yourself.
Think about how you have already used new ideas to
improve your life, or solve a problem. You were stuck.
Then insight and finally breakthrough. You can use this
experience to become even better at making new ideas
successful.

Look at how practically creative people think and
work. Learn more about how new ideas are generated,
developed and popularised. Learn about the psychology
of the innovator and the shape of innovation from start to
finish and back to new beginnings.

Pay attention to the life stories of the ideas and
innovations that surround you and how scientific discovery
blends with human imagination to produce revolution.

Becoming a creative problem-solver – an innovator
– is about getting better at transforming ideas into

improvement. And becoming bolder at bringing revolutionary ideas to life in the real world.

You can create better new ideas worth bringing to life. You can nurture new ideas from insight through to innovation. It is human nature to make connections between existing ideas (or facts) and use them to create new ideas (or discoveries).

You can become better at moving from dissatisfaction with the way things are, to critique and complain, to seek better, and become bolder, simpler and smarter.

Nurturing your creative genius

If there are no new ideas, there is no innovation. And if there is no creativity, there are no new ideas. There is little truth in the criticism that all ideas are cheap. Or that having a good idea is always easy. Everyone *is* creative, but not everyone is equally creative. And not everyone is creative in exactly the same way, or as often, or as effectively. Highly creative people *behave* differently, and you can too.

Frequency – Continually develop your creativity.
Key participants – You.
Innovation rating – Innovation6

The world's first non-stick frying pan was created after the wife of a French engineer suggested the substance he'd been using on his fishing gear might help prevent burnt food. Her insight led to a series of experiments that, in turn, led to the founding of the company Tefal which, which within five years was selling one million frying pans every month.

The substance he used was the result of an accident. It was discovered by an American chemist in New Jersey. He failed to make a better chemical for refrigerators and instead created Teflon. Two old ideas created one new idea. At Tefal, an idea-hungry culture has grown up around this innovation tradition so that half its sales are now based on products created less than two years ago. The company's future depends on many more happy accidents.

Objective

The psychology of individual creativity is about at least three different things. First, creativity is about thinking differently. Second, creativity is about feeling differently. Third, creativity is about focusing, or committing, differently. All three are important to practical creativity.

Thinking differently

The cognitive (thinking) side of creativity is about generating new ideas. This can be a new answer to a question. It can be lots of different answers to the same question. It can be something that is weird, or something that's simply never been seen before. It can be something that you've never thought before, even if other people have had the same thought. It must be different, something that is not the obvious, or the usual, or the traditional idea or concept.

Feeling differently

The affective (emotional) side of creativity is about the way you see the world. The highly creative tend to interact with the world differently so that their choices, answers and solutions are naturally different. If you care about solving something that others think is impossible, or unimportant, you are more likely to find creative solutions. Everyone feels slightly differently but these differences can often be hidden away or locked up by rules, traditions, habits and convention.

Focusing differently

The conative (effortful) side of creativity is about willpower. The true parents of creativity are curiosity and necessity. Highly creative people, or people behaving in a highly creative way, become obsessed with newness. Sometimes they want novelty because it pleases them. On other occasions they need novelty to achieve another goal, not for its own sake but because there is really no other way of getting the desired results. The difference is important.

Challenge

Becoming more creative is about recognising how creativity thinks, feels and focuses. Not everyone is equally good, or bad, at each. There are those who can create an idea seemingly effortlessly while others seem to struggle even when lives, or livelihoods, depend upon it. Yet, creativity is more process than mystery. You can become more creative and share those lessons with others.

Collecting ideas make sense because all new ideas are made of other ideas – new, old, ancient, modern, stupid, smart or dumb. Instead of picking up the proven idea, you reach for the unproven idea. Rather than learning about the kind of idea that you always choose, you learn about the kind of idea you would normally dismiss. You plug yourself into the energy of new ideas from radio, television, the internet, new people and new situations. You become an idea magpie.

Transforming ideas is about exploring the elasticity of the ideas you've collected. Every idea can be combined with another idea to form something new. Every idea can be made bigger or smaller. Every idea can be diluted or concentrated, multiplied or divided, exaggerated or understated. You can reverse the assumption or reverse the implementation. You can make any idea prettier, uglier, stronger, weaker, longer, thinner, higher, lower or faster. You become an idea magician.

Exploring ideas is about seeing what difference the new idea could make. If you replace an existing idea with this new idea, what would happen? What do you think would change? This part of the creative process is still in your head. You haven't spent anything except mental effort. This kind of imaginative experiment expands your creativity. You develop creative reflexes and skills. You gain a working (conceptual) knowledge of the idea. You better understand situations and opportunities.

Nurturing ideas moves a little further from the conceptual to the real world. You start to underline ideas that interest you. Maybe you just love something about the new idea. Or you can see some valuable difference that the new idea could make. You jot down the mechanics of the idea on paper, a whiteboard, a few notes to yourself or you float it to people via informal chat on- or offline. This is about letting some of your ideas do a little growing up, feeding them and interacting with them.

This part isn't really about having useful ideas. This part is about having enough ideas that are crazy enough or imaginative enough to be useful. If the idea is too safe then it probably doesn't have the power to significantly improve the situation. If the idea is just an extension to the way things have always been done, then it is less likely to get you to change the way things are done for the better.

You need to generate new ideas before you can select between those new ideas. And it makes sense to create lots of new ideas so you can throw them together to create exactly the kind of idea you need for a particular purpose. Or find new ideas to provide opportunities to a better purpose.

Context

Creativity is a process. The internal creative process can be helped or hindered by the external creative process. The flow of ideas through an organisation may be too slow and too judgemental to bring you sufficient raw materials for new insights. Your workspace may be too dull or negative to encourage imaginative adventure or play. The people who surround you may be anti-idea, anti-novelty, or just so similar that you rarely hear anything you didn't previously hear or know.

People in positions of authority often favour order over chaos. Organised people tend to squeeze out divergent possibilities because they want to get on with convergent opportunities. Unfortunately, time and cost pressure often also discourages people from playing and exploring new ideas needed for successful innovation. The truth is that progress depends on stability *and* instability.

There is a danger that people develop a kind of learning helplessness. They wait for formal permission or training or resources before they start to be creative. Or they hide their creativity for fear of embarrassment, punishment or simply being blocked. If only creativity from senior managers, or outside experts, is rewarded, then why be creative at the bottom or middle of the organisation?

It's tempting to self-censor your ability to do something new or beautiful because of bad experiences, because you don't believe you are creative, or because you think there's only one right answer. In reality, there are endless answers to countless subjective and objective questions about what is better. Nothing is fixed. Most of everything we take for granted in our modern lives has been invented or discovered by the creative dissatisfaction of our predecessors.

Believing in just one best answer is a habit as well as a personality trait. It's encouraged by formal schooling. The safety from fitting into the group by living, and thinking, according to an accepted normal tradition is attractive to many people. In extreme cases, only the incurably creative retain their everyday ability to generate divergent ideas. They are the novelty outliers, the future builders.

Success

You will start to love new ideas. You'll feel, focus and think differently from your colleagues. People come to you for suggestions because you have a reputation for being original. You're more likely to be the first to introduce breakthroughs and bizarre facts to friends, family and workgroup. You are more likely to be the early adopter than the laggard.

You become a novelty outlier. Innovation depends on actions and ideas that are new. You can't extend the limits of possibility without someone doing what has never been done before. There's sometimes temporary safety in the middle but there is nothing *better* in the median.

As you explore and play with ideas, your ability to *be* creative will increase. As your ability to be creative develops, your creative confidence will also increase. This confidence – known as self-efficacy – is a mark of those who are reliably and highly creative. The advantage in nurturing creativity is a self-perpetuating cycle. The more creative you feel, the more creative you act.

Stimulation is necessary to provide you with the raw material of creativity, but you also know where to find isolation to start processing your new ideas. Move between places with problems – which can spark insights – and places with ideas, thoughts and theories that are *new to you*. As you play with the space between problems and ideas, you will discover and develop your innate creativity.

Innovator's measure of success

→ You understand what makes people more creatively productive.

→ Creative habits are developed that keep new ideas flowing.

→ Self-efficacy (or confidence) in your individual creativity increases.

→ Your fluency grows in creating original opinions and non-obvious answers.

→ There is a time (and place) for creative stimulation and isolation.

Pitfalls

You might mistakenly think practical creativity (or innovation) can be learned only from a book. Or that practical creativity can be developed in isolation from the real world. You might take part in creativity training that leaves you with the impression that you are *not* creative because you don't know the specific techniques that are being taught. There's a danger that efforts to formalise innovation take the initiative away from practical everyday creativity. Your confidence and commitment to solving real-world problems matters much more than specific techniques or tools.

Innovator's checklist

▨ **Plug yourself into novelty.** When you catch yourself dismissing the latest fashion or fad, stop that dismissive response and embrace the untested. Doing six impossible things before breakfast tends to come after consuming 60 original ideas for dinner (see creative problem-solving on page 158).

▨ **Store and play with new ideas**. Stick things on noticeboards. Write ideas in notebooks. Tear out photos. Highlight sentences

in books. Draw thoughts on napkins and in margins. Draw
connections between concepts, people and places. Join ideas
to other ideas. Create idea lucky dips and grab bags with
randomly acquired magazines, toys, tools, objects and subjects.

▓ **Move between stimulation and isolation.** Your brain needs
injections of the revolutionary and mind-blowing. You need the
provocation of problems. Ideas spilling over. Concepts bursting
out. Noise. Music. Art. Experience. Your over-stimulated brain
must then find respite. Your unconscious must reorder and
remake. Let your mind index and connect.

▓ **Find new communities and people.** Explore other scenes. Go to
new places. Wander through your workplace. Start conversations.
Create online photo galleries. Browse academic websites. Read
the magazines about other professions or hobbies. Travel.
Experience (see networks for innovation on page 235).

▓ **Stretch your imagination.** Use one idea to find your way to
something more extreme. What if you only had 10 minutes
to find a solution? What if you had a billion dollars to invest?
What could you do if skills were not a limitation? Which
magical power would you choose?

Related ideas

In *The Innovator's DNA*, Clayton Christensen, Hal Gregersen and
colleagues, interviewed famous innovators. The results suggest five
behavioural discovery skills: associating, questioning, observing,
networking, and experimenting. The authors offer a disclaimer
that engaging in discovery skills does not guarantee success. Others
may produce better innovation, or mistakes may be made. That's
why innovators move beyond discovering new ideas to learning to
grind their way from insight to innovation (see page 81).

One more thing

Intel was the poster-child for paranoid innovation. It saw waves
of mobile computing coming and yet Qualcomm left it behind.

How could this happen? The way that innovative thinking is nurtured is one answer: Qualcomm employees are rewarded for registering new patents. An entire wall of its headquarters is filled with patent certificates. It focuses less on formal programmes for innovation and more on self-organised ideas sessions over meal breaks. One such approach – called FLUX or 'Forward Looking User Experience' – has no full-time staff but has already led to 45 patents.

Do this now!

Spend 10 minutes finding out why other people love a new idea that you hate

Maybe everyone is talking about Twitter, drag car racing, baseball or stand-up comedy and you think they're a waste of time. Perhaps, you don't see the point of reality TV, fashion shows, video games or twerking. You don't understand why your partner, lover, friend, colleague, child or boss spends so much time on something so boring, silly, obvious, banal, complicated or stupid. So try and find out.

Seeing what others do not see

Before innovation – or practical creativity – there is insight. You must see the world differently. You need to see gaps between what is and what can be. As an innovator, the ability to see what others cannot see is valuable. You may see puzzles to be solved or the final piece of the puzzle. You see further or differently.

Frequency – Every problem. Every opportunity.
Key participants – You.
Innovation rating:****

According to George Yancopoulos – the chief scientific officer of Regeneron – he got into the drugs business because he had an insight. He is a drug hunter who has figured out how to develop new treatments for less money. In an industry where big players spend $10 billion for each new drug, his company spends less than $750 million. Its biggest success helps prevent blindness in adults.

Regeneron's success has been about stringing together new insights. It focuses on increasing its understanding of the disease and identifying side-effects before committing to particular new drugs. It uses hard-won insights as proven building blocks for new innovations. The company reengineered lab mice with human DNA to make test results more reliable and so reducing time to market. Its newest trick is to find human mutations that are resistant to disease and then turn them into drug treatments.

Objective

Innovation can start with wanting what does not yet exist – and finding a solution – or seeing what does not yet exist – and finding an opportunity. You can solve old problems with new ideas in new ways. You can solve new problems with old ideas in new ways. You need a series of insights to make those new combinations from opportunity to solution.

Thinking style is about how you approach situations and solve problems. We all have to adapt to situations and find solutions to problems but we don't all adapt and solve in the same way. You will see different opportunities depending on your perspective, knowledge and personality. The various opportunities will seem more or less attractive depending on how you assess costs and advantages.

Domain creativity is about whether you are creative generally – in all situations – or creative in specific situations. The evidence suggests that most innovation comes from domain-specific creativity. This is because you are more likely to make an original contribution if you know more about the situation, have more situation relevant skills and do more thinking about the situation.

Insight paradox is about the relative benefits and costs of creative diversity. Having people who know lots about a situation – experience – is efficient at getting the job done well according to existing rules but is not so good at creating better rules. You need to inject diversity into the situation or people won't see new problems worth solving. They will be guided by habit rather than possibility.

Insights are magical but not magic. Most valuable insights come from people who have paid a price to understand something better. They reach into the detail. They spend time with a problem until they can recognise a new solution. Or they gain solution skills until they can apply them creatively. Insights emerge from a mixture of thinking style, skills, knowledge and experience.

Context

Problem-insight precedes solution-insight. Someone has to see a problem before they start to solve the problem. Solving your own problem can motivate the effort required. It can also give deep insights because you know – or want to know – the intricacies of how the problem works. You may be dependent on solution-insights from other people who know less about the problem.

Solving problems for other people can also be motivational when you have solution-insights to offer. You take your expertise and apply it to a new problem. What appeared difficult to solve without your knowledge can be easy to solve with your know-how. You may be dependent on problem-insights from other people who know less about the solutions but much more about the problem.

To see what others do not see can be about looking at new things. It can be about looking at old things in new ways. It can be about combining new and old things in new ways. It can also be about being motivated enough to follow the shape of a problem until you find the shape of a solution. Or about finding the people who are motivated to poke, pry and play until valuable insight arises.

Challenge

This flow from individual problem-insight to more collective solution-insight is important. You can do more to make the first insight more likely by developing your inner (creative) genius. The original problem-insight can lead to ideas for solving the problem. Your original problem-insight needs to be shared with other people to find more problem-insights, situation-insights and solution-insights.

You can hunt insights alone. You can make lists of what you know and don't know to solve your problem. You can ask people what you don't know. You can use your problem-insight to find new uses for the solution-skills of others. You can also start to recruit other insight-hunters to your cause. As you create more specific solution-insights you will need people who understand and go beyond.

All people have problems. In most situations, there are more problem spotters than problem solvers. Some people have problem-insights but far fewer people work their way from a vague problem-insight into a specific solution-insight. Some see the problem but don't see how it's their problem.

As a practical creative, you can move from experiencing life problems to improving the lives of others. As an innovator, you can transform the gap you've seen into something worthwhile. This is another way of seeing what others do not see. You see the value in making something better.

Success

You're getting better at seeing what others don't see when you reach different conclusions from the group naturally. You can get to something beyond the standard opinions. You can get to somewhere completely different although you all start in what appears to be the same situation. You have new information buzzing around your head that jumps into the problem-solving process. You are willing to jump ahead of the trend or take an entirely new viewpoint. Seeing differently is now a habit.

Innovator's measure of success

- Understand your unique viewpoint.
- Use your unique viewpoint to find and develop problem-insights.
- Compare your viewpoint with various traditional and alternative viewpoints.
- Embrace different viewpoints as a way of making and extending your insights.
- Join (or create) networks of people who care about your unique insights.

Pitfalls

You can get so good at seeing things differently that you can't explain your viewpoint to others. When you share your insight with other people, your original insight can become lost in a muddle of how other people perceive things. You can give up too soon on what made your insight valuable. You can also be too narrowly focused to make your insight workable. You will need – as ever – to try and blend insights into something that can solve a real-world problem you care about. It's tempting to think you have to wait until you know everything before following your gut feeling. It's equally tempting to think that the hard-won perspective of expertise has nothing to teach you.

Innovator's checklist

■ Embrace your ability to see things differently. Everyone has a unique perspective. Your place in the world. Your job. Your upbringing. Your route to work. Your hobbies. Your obsessions. Your peculiarities. Your ignorance. All of these can be valuable in creating innovation (see design thinking on page 207).

■ Identify your problem-insights. Pay attention to what's happening around you. Use your smartphone. Keep a notebook. Take photos of stuff that doesn't work. Record videos of what you love. Chat to people with problems. Think about how things could be better.

■ Compare your viewpoint. Look for the differences between it and how others see the situation. Find others who see things differently to fill in the gaps and challenge your insights. Discover know-how you need now. Use your insights to spark new insights from other people.

Related ideas

Use the models in the toolkit (see page 147) to find new ways of seeing problems and situations. You can follow the problem into the conceptual world and then into proven ways of solving problems that are similar (see page 161). As a leader of innovation, you can help (or support) your people to use open innovation to look outside your own resources and perspective (see page 223).

One more thing

Nikolaos Papanikolopoulo always liked to take things apart and find out how they worked. His obsessive need to understand complex things led him to robotics. And his weird persistence pulled him towards insights about where and how to help people with amazing robots.

His insights about how gathering better information could save lives in dangerous situations led ultimately to the Throwbot. The Throwbot can be thrown into action in toxic or dangerous situations and right itself no matter how it lands. It is remote-controlled, near silent and broadcasts video to a smartphone display. New insights have led to mother-ship robots that control other robots as teams, to hoverbots, amphibious robots and to real-life transformers.

Part of Papanikolopoulo's secret as an innovator is to disassemble things (and situations) and then reassemble them. He breaks things down to fix them (better). Another trick is to combine his expertise (in maths, engineering and artificial intelligence) with the curiosity of kids, ambition of undergraduates, near expertise of doctoral students and needs of real people with real problems.

Do this now!

Spend 10 minutes finding some regular space in your schedule for nurturing your creativity

You need time to play, discover, solve and learn. You could plan a specific time. Monday morning to start your week full of new ideas or Wednesday afternoon to give yourself a mid-week creative injection. Perhaps, just commit to complete one of these action topics daily or weekly. It's an effective way of turning these ideas about innovation into your own ability to make new ideas useful.

Becoming a more powerful innovator

Practical creativity – or innovation – can be developed by improving the match between you and your situation. Innovation also needs you to be dissatisfied with the way things are. You need to travel to the limits and want to go further. The great innovators want more, better, faster. They take us forward.

Frequency – At the beginning, then regularly.
Key participants – First you. Then, everyone.
Innovation rating:**

The CEO of CarMax is hungry for suggestions. He seeks, encourages and transforms dissatisfaction with how things are – even if the way things are is successful. There are more than 100 stores with more than 18,000 people working there. A winner of awards for customer service and best workplace, the culture is driven by competition against disliked traditions of the car industry.

CarMax only happened because of a suggestion from a creative outsider. The CEO of Circuit City hired a consultant to explore future possibilities. The consultant came up with the idea for revolutionising the whole experience of buying a car. As it happens, the old company no longer exists, but the new company – later spun off – has revenues of $90 billion. And the ideas keep flowing through town-hall meetings with a team who are perpetually dissatisfied with the ways things are.

Objective

Innovators go to the edge of what is possible and then jump beyond. Or at least they try. Sometimes they fall or fail but the attempt is made. Almost every leap into the unknown is valuable. You learn. Or someone else learns from your struggle. Your next attempt is informed by previous attempts. You can leap from experiment to experiment into new insights, problems and ideas.

Satisfaction drives mastery	Dissatisfaction energises innovation
Willing to master traditional skills.	Unwilling to accept traditional limitations.
Endless passion for deep learning.	Restless desire for novel experiences.
Finding your intellectual homeland.	Discovering your creative fantasyland.
Fulfilment and flow from how-things-are.	Frustration and obsession with things-as-can-be.
Looking (and feeling) like a natural.	Feeling (and looking) like a rebel.

Satisfaction drives mastery while dissatisfaction energises innovation. At any time, you can become annoyed, frustrated, fed-up and unwilling to accept old ways of doing things. You can be dissatisfied with something about which you are, pretty much, ignorant.

The benefit of not knowing much is that you may not accept traditional constraints. But the difficulty of not knowing much is that you don't have the skills or the detailed knowledge to find a solution. You may waste time, and resources, solving what is already solved rather than pushing beyond.

Context

Innovation, or practical creativity, emerges from many different personality traits. You might look like a caricature of a creative person and still not create anything new or valuable. It's also entirely possible to create something new, and valuable, without its value being recognised.

Rembrandt was dismissed by his peers but then placed above them by art historians. Findings from the 18th-century experiments of Gregor Mendel, considered the founder of genetic science, were rejected until 20th-century scientists realised the significance of his work.

Innovation requires fit between personality, preparation, place and problem. People have different general levels, and styles, of problem-solving, analysis and insight. Yet generally creative isn't quite the same as specific creative contribution. Motivation to *do* the creative work is necessary. The most gifted creative thinker produces nothing without the willpower to move from insight to innovation.

Some people have the ability to stick with a task regardless of their interest or progress. Others need to be motivated by the specific activity (the work) or a specific objective. Refusal to quit can be useful but not when accompanied by refusal to adapt. Innovators accept doing necessary work to overcome the unnecessary constraints they reject.

You must be single-mindedly open-minded. This means being focused without being blinkered. You are ready to shift your goals when desirable. You change methods when helpful. Think of Stan Lee, at Marvel Comics, who started as a perfectionist writing each word for every script and panel. Eventually his desire to create the world's first comic book universe forced him to share scripting with other writers and artists and allowed a super-hero, mutant-powered revolution.

Challenge

The trick to deliberately becoming a more powerful innovator is to understand how different parts of practical creativity work together. Innovation emerges when new solutions are applied to a valuable problem *and* the new solution becomes the new improved tradition. The right innovator has to find the right problem. The right audience must recognise the right solution and use it in the right way. Every new idea has a habitable space, somewhere it can thrive and grow.

Successful innovators tend to have practical intelligence, openness to experience, freedom from constraints, insight into the underlying mechanisms of how something works, and flexibility in how they think. They are often very independent, with obsessive commitment to their quest and unusually high energy levels. They have highs and lows, needing isolation and then stimulation.

They are on the edge of orthodoxy and may want to prove they are right. You can't innovate without seeing flaws in the way things are done. You can't make new ideas popular unless you are willing to fight for your new ideas. Every innovator has a series of making points – long before they prove their point through changing the way something is done. They need to fall into (or in love) with a scene, a situation, a community, and discover a purpose to drive them beyond mastery to transformation.

Some of the path to innovation is out of your control. Genetics and parents are not yet the choice of those born. Yet they have an impact. Being the eldest in a large family seems to increase creativity. Not too much and not too little parental support is important. As is access to the domain – or situation – where your kind of creativity is sparked and then found useful.

When they find their passion, innovators are helped by finding a small group of peers. The tight-knit group provides emotional support and constructive conflict. The innovators' club can contribute informally with missing knowledge, puzzle pieces and a way of imaginatively testing new ideas. The peers can offer part of the context for changing the game. The match between innovation-space and potential innovator changes what is possible.

Success

Finding your innovation-space is part of you finding your inner creative genius. You need an emotional connection. You need a situation that motivates the effort to gain new insights. For innovation, not all environments are equal. You want to become better at matching your aspirations (dreams, desires, ambitions) and abilities (skills, knowledge, willpower) with the most fruitful fields for innovation. Your success will depend on finding the right place and time.

It's worth looking around for a field, industry or market sufficiently open to new ideas. You can recognise a healthy field-of-focus by its hunger for novelty, the diversity of opinions, willingness to experiment, and hunger and potential for growth. Rigidity, hierarchy, lack of resources, missing expertise and prejudice, on any basis, will make it harder for your new ideas to make a difference.

To be useful, every new idea must become part of an existing web of ideas and people. Human systems shape the way that ideas are accepted, used or rejected. Your attempts to innovate will be more successful if you can contribute to idea webs that you understand. Look at all the people who will have to use your idea or change to accommodate your idea. Think about the direction and speed of change to the idea-web outside your control. You are more likely to create powerful, popular innovations when you can see the workings of the system you need to succeed.

Innovator's measures of success

➤ You recognise that practical innovation is blended from traits, actions and circumstance.

➤ Find the innovation-space that motivates you to master the fundamentals.

➤ Locate an innovation-space which you feel driven to transform.

➤ Assess the idea-hunger of the target industries, markets and professions.

➤ Identify the barriers to your being accepted as an innovator.

➤ Understand the culture, society and history of new ideas in your problem-space.

➤ You know how new ideas are introduced, judged, shared, rewarded and improved.

Pitfalls

Believing innovation is only about new ideas is a mistake. There are old solutions to new problems and new solutions to old problems. New ideas can also create new problems. The smart innovator explores whether a radically new idea is really worthwhile. Consider what happens if you don't find a new solution. If the cost of not having innovation is low then perhaps no innovation is necessary. Or perhaps there's a different way of achieving the same goal by using an idea that is new to you but that already works elsewhere.

Innovator's checklist

- Where do you feel naturally strong and comfortable? In which subjects? In what industry? Solving what kind of problems? Doing what is second nature is an advantage when trying to improve whatever is being done. You can acquire skills, helpers and resources more easily.

- Look for a match between opportunities to innovate and your personal attributes. How long would you be willing to work on a creative solution? Are you willing (and able) to work with the people that are needed for your innovation to work?

- Ask around to better understand the level of openness to new ideas. Is the culture idea toxic, idea wasteful, idea friendly or idea hungry? Are there any prejudices (or stereotypes) that will make people less likely to listen? Are there legal or cultural roadblocks? (see creating an innovation culture on page 35).

- Find your innovation peers. You will need mentors to give you wisdom, friendly critics to test your ideas, and competition from people as driven as you are.

- Locate well-known problems or limitations. How have previous solutions been attempted? When were the last big breakthroughs? Where did the innovations come from? What stopped people going further? Where did previous innovators get stuck or blocked?

Related ideas

Creativity, like any other skill, benefits from *deliberate practice*. There are several innovation learning curves. Learning enough about a situation to imagine solutions and perform imaginative experiments against your mental model. Learning about possible skills and technologies that you can move from imaginary to real solutions. And learning about shaping the dynamic of innovation, people and solutions. Deliberate practice involves gaining basic skills and know-how, then improving those skills before jumping to more challenging levels with more advanced skills and knowledge.

One more thing

The hands of the best spine surgeon in the world are robotic. With a success rate twice that of human hands, the Renaissance product from Mazor Robotics is a thing of wonder. It makes 3D scans of damaged spines and lets the surgeon design a surgical blueprint before completing the planned surgery from a mount placed above the patient. The company deliberately nurtures creative collaboration with an executive given the role of devil's advocate, a weekly all-employee meeting, and a tradition of not disagreeing via email but doing so face-to-face.

Do this now!

Spend 10 minutes being inspired by people doing real things in the real world

Use a search engine to find video of people playing or working. If you're a publisher, you might look for how people talk about books. If you work for an airline, watch people planning flights, holidays or work trips. Look at what drives them crazy and what they're crazy about. Can you feel their pain? Or share in their joy? Forward the video with a comment to a friend or colleague. See something new.

Giving up old ideas for better ideas

If you need to get to never-been-done, the path may not be obvious. It's tempting to embrace only what you already know even if you know that what you know doesn't get you anywhere better. We like our habits; they may not help but at least we don't have to do any hard thinking or uncomfortable learning. It may feel easier to do the old, old thing than the new, new thing.

Frequency – Each time progress starts to slow down.
Key participants – First you. Then people who are stuck.
Innovation rating:**

A Kodak engineer, asked by his supervisor, invented the first digital camera. They combined a new semiconductor with a television and data cassette to take a 0.01 megapixel photo. It took Kodak 16 years to get a single dollar from the invention: a one-off sale of a spy camera after a request from the US government. Kodak ignored the new idea because it didn't play nicely with its existing cash ideas.

Apple was first to market with a digital camera that worked with home computers. Kodak was second to market, and created a network to popularise the digital camera. Microsoft built the kiosks. Kinko's served customers. IBM created a photo network. HP invented colour inkjets for printing. Yet, Kodak refused give up its old idea and so couldn't adapt to the new idea as fast as its competitors.

Objective

You can have amazing insights and remarkable inventions but if they involve (painful) change many people will ignore them. Innovator lovers tend to assume that all innovation is good and that all innovation is equally good for everyone. The truth about innovation is that most new ideas involve some kind of pain but that not all those pains are equal or equally distributed.

There are four pains to a new idea. There is *necessary pain* –
the effort to develop and make room for the new (better) idea.
Some will experience *unnecessary pain* – avoidable mistakes and
uncaring application of new ideas. There is *industry pain* where
existing structures and processes change in response to newer
ideas and technologies. There is also *people pain* where humans
expend energy and effort, lose prestige, jobs and wealth, or
stretch to new ideas.

You can have unnecessary or necessary people pain. You can
cause necessary or unnecessary industry pain. Some pay the price
for smart new ideas willingly hoping for something better. Others
recognise when plans for new ideas are flawed and not worth
the pain. Only dumb innovators assume all change is good. As
a smart innovator, you can try to make sure the price is worth
paying.

Some of the pain of a new idea comes from giving up old ideas.
Letting go can be mentally exhausting and psychologically
uncomfortable. It can be emotionally simpler to increase
commitment to what doesn't work rather than suffer cognitive
dissonance. Groups of all kinds can become more extreme in
their faith *after* the obvious failure of their guiding predictions,
plans, prophecies, principles, politics and policies. Some people
prefer losing to quitting.

Some of the pain of a new idea comes from *not* giving up old
ideas. This can be caused by habitual commitment to the way
things were done. It can be tempting to defend old ideas when
they have brought us success. And equally easy to attack new
ideas because they disrupt situations we like or simply because
they are new. Pain comes because the world moves on to a new
idea and that new idea will make life more difficult and competition fiercer *until* we adapt. Quitting can be winning.

If people do not make room for new ideas there is nowhere for
those new ideas to fit. If there is nowhere for those new ideas
to fit, then they cannot be tested. Even if there is evidence for
them, that evidence will not be sufficient to make the new idea
welcome. The trick is to make space for new ideas to be played

with, considered and nurtured. And to say goodbye to unhelpful old ideas.

Context

Often new ideas are rejected or accepted as though those are the only choices. This can lead to new ideas being rejected or accepted before they are ready. Where they are rejected, amazing new ideas have no power to help people adapt or improve. Where they are too easily accepted, dumb or ugly new ideas are given too much power before they are ready. So, understanding the dynamic is helpful.

People depend on habit and tradition. Habitual thinking and action helps to conserve mental and emotional energy. Habits simplify decision-making. Habits can help us to work with others because of accepted behaviours, priorities, clothes, language, logic and priorities. Some conventions are conscious, followed for utility or conformity. They can help us fit in or complete specific tasks.

Other conventions are instinctive or subconsciously followed. We humans are not aware of everything we are doing or thinking. Sometimes we judge events as more important just because we can remember them (the availability heuristic) or experience short-lived emotion that can dramatically change whether risks appear high or low (the affect heuristic). These short-cuts are not necessarily rational or irrational but they change the nature of decisions *outside* of deliberate logic.

As an innovator, you need to be aware of how traditions, habits and bias can act as barriers to accepting new ideas. It's also useful to know how to overcome barriers to better ideas while retaining the ability to be selective. People avoid uncertain decisions and underestimate how much to adapt to new circumstances. They have a bias towards things staying the same, a tendency to take more risks to avoid losses than to increase gains, and get more stubborn under pressure.

You can use this kind of knowledge about human behaviour to shape the way new ideas are presented. This is helpful to *selling* (smart) new ideas and increasing the likelihood that they are adopted. Or that certain (dumb) new ideas are rejected. At a deeper level, as a supporter of practical creativity, you can make others aware that such dynamics exist. In this way, new ideas can be more productively explored, developed and adopted. The group members learn to overcome their own bias.

Challenge

Letting go of old ideas is about recognising the relentless need – and opportunity – for adaptation. You won't know at first which ideas need to be abandoned or which ideas will replace them. But you will know that progress, improvement and even survival will require some of *what* is done and some of *how* it is done to be changed. Many beliefs, mechanisms and goals can be replaced with better versions or at least with editions that *fit* better with the demands of the current environment.

High adaptability	Low adaptability
Take risks to make gains.	Take risks to avoid losses.
Uncertainty prompts new learning.	Certainty from old learning.
Explore to increase options.	Exploit to increase profits.
Driven by future opportunities.	Driven by conformity.
Learning by experimentation.	Learning by tradition.

People are more likely to seek new ideas when they are driven by desirable future opportunities. The leader who emphasises the desirable future is more likely to naturally engage the creativity of the group. There are others driven more by negative outcomes that they wish to avoid but these risks are based more often on gambling more on old ideas. Creating urgency around avoidance of something bad (the burning platform) can close more minds than it opens.

To make room for new learning, there needs to be space for unlearning. Some of this unlearning is about one behaviour replacing another behaviour. You start to do something new and this becomes the new habit. Past behaviours are forgotten. Old skills are lost. New behaviours may be copied from other people because they are attractive, successful, influential or simply in authority. Some new behaviours arise because situations change so much that the old behaviour isn't possible. You may be blocked from doing something old or attracted to something new. Action first, thinking later.

Some unlearning is one kind of thinking replacing another kind. Available facts may change. Theories explaining available facts change. Or ambitions, priorities and objectives that guide thinking change. You think in new (or different) ways and this wipes out the previous way. New thinking may come first with new action later. Transformation can be rapid when new ideas and behaviours combine.

Success

The trick is to recognise that new actions do not automatically follow new ideas. You are prepared to give up old ideas so that you can benefit from new ideas. You leave room for the new behaviours that make better ideas worthwhile – and actively look for changes that flow from new ideas. New experiences are embraced – even when uninvited – because they can build personal flexibility.

The innovator is able to adapt to ever-shifting consequences – in part because the innovative mind is only loosely committed to any particular method, process or structure. Rejecting any ultimate truth – or fixed answer – allows you to fluidly move to better when you find better.

Learn what is done. Learn why people are doing things the way they are done. Question the linkages and assumptions.

You will look *behind* rules and procedures. You will become better at examining the relationships between objectives, actions and outcomes. Any of these are interchangeable. If you find lazy assumptions, there may be room for an upgrade to logic or action. Training is an opportunity to find out what is not known rather than passively conforming to one-best-way forever.

Innovator's measure of success

- You recognise that existing ideas may be replaced by new ideas.
- You know the limitations of learning and the necessity of unlearning.
- There is a working assumption that all assumptions can be questioned.
- Learning focuses on fluid thinking ahead of static knowledge.

Pitfalls

Some people are so new-idea hungry they have a kind of novelty fetish. These change addicts are not as interested in whether the new idea makes anything better as they are in the newness itself. This makes them excellent conduits for different approaches but unreliable filters for the utility of ideas. You want to make room for new ideas without gutting systems that already work. An uncontrollable desire for difference has risks. It can divert creativity and resources from solving valuable problems.

Innovator's checklist

- Identify assumptions behind old ideas *and* new ideas.

- Use new experiences to develop fluid actions and behaviour. Look at how you usually respond to new events. Do you always react in the same way? Do you keep doing what doesn't work? Do you act without thinking? Are you happy with the results of habitual actions? Have you learned new lessons that have not changed your actions?

- Explore new opportunities made possible by new ideas (technology or methods). Are there possible improvements that were ignored? Are there isolated changes in one area that

cannot work without complementary changes in another area?
Are new ideas crowded out by old priorities? How can you stop
doing old things to make room for new things?

■ Develop creative habits to counteract anti-creative habits that
tend to solidify with time. Learn how to use controversy in
constructive ways (see page 231) that make room for new ideas
by creating alternatives.

■ Study the real lives of innovators. Speak with people who have
made breakthroughs in your workplace, industry or community.
Many people overestimate the importance of keeping the rules –
and taking no risks – in explaining the success of others. There is
a gap between official best practice and unofficial practices that
work in the real world (see Part 5 on Innovator's turning points).

Related ideas

According to Kirton's A-I theory, one reason people clash about
new ideas is they think differently about newness. Some people like
to make things better while other people like to do things differently. Each group is more comfortable with people who share the
same thinking style. People who like incremental improvement
tend to create incremental improvement cultures and distrust
radical innovators. Radical innovators tend to seek out radical
innovation cultures and clash with incremental improvers. They
may both want improvement but clash over style, scale and speed.

One more thing

The netbook phenomenon lasted just five years. A mere 67
months from the time that Asus released its first EeePC to the
announcement that it had ceased production. Easy to learn, easy
to work, easy to play and fantastically easy to sell. By 2011, the
new idea of tablets – led by the mighty iPad – had replaced the
old idea of netbooks in the hearts and homes of consumers. Asus
was forced to either surf the wave into tablets (which it's still
trying) or be stranded by new customer tastes.

Do this now!

Devote 10 minutes to questioning assumptions about the way things have to be

People often accept, without thinking, that a bad situation is unchangeable or that a good situation cannot be improved. So ask questions: was it different in the past? Does evidence support the way things are being done? Who is doing it differently? Why are we doing it this way? What is stopping the situation being reversed? Change things on paper and see whether it's worth doing in the real world.

two

Leading innovators

'Passion is one great force that unleashes creativity, because if you're passionate about something, then you're more willing to take risks.'
Yo-Yo Ma, Cellist

You may be the person doing the creative work. Or you may be leading the creative efforts of others. You may need to inspire insight, ideas or innovation and get people to work together even when those new ideas are strange, misunderstood, challenging or threatening. This is leadership.

There are different roles to be played at different times. Sometimes you're the *creator* who comes up with the new idea. You may inspire other people to have the new ideas or set the problems that need to be solved.

Sometimes you're the *collaborator*, working to make the idea useful in the real world. Or you may be responsible for bringing people together who can collaborate to make the idea useful or popular.

Innovation works best as a collective activity. You can build a better, bigger brain by connecting the creativity and passion of many different kinds of people.

Skills are needed, as is expertise. Points of view and knowledge about particular situations. Access to resources, equipment, money, time, permission or the work required to actually build, implement and sustain the innovation in the real world.

As you organise people for innovation, you can create an innovation culture that allows your group to create more valuable, beautiful things. As an innovator, you can move towards a kind of competitive paradise working with people to make the world better.

Building a better, bigger brain

No individual can have all the answers. Even a creative genius cannot have all the best solutions to all the world's problems. Everyone has something to offer to the process of innovation. You'll need problems to solve, insights into solutions, people to make the ideas work, and people to use the innovations in the real world. You want to build a better brain, a bigger brain.

Frequency – Learn at the start. Refer to regularly.
Key participants – First you. Then, everyone.
Innovation rating – Innovation6

Once upon a time, Google was famous for giving engineers 20% of their time to work on any project that they wanted. They didn't have to justify the use of this paid time. They could choose to pool their 20% with others to develop innovations outside the corporate plan. Google-time helped the company launch new experimental products and services. It also helped them to explore the potential of trends and technologies before investing in billion-dollar acquisitions like YouTube.

The new CEO has made it harder to use 20% time. New performance management systems push people to use their extra time to work on formal projects. The plan is focused on priorities set by the CEO. Experimentation has a formally sanctioned home in 'moon-shot' projects at the top secret Google X laboratory.

The evolution of innovation at Google is not necessarily smart or dumb, it just has consequences. More of the brain is being directed and organised from above than in the past. It is more top down and also more portfolio driven. There is less opportunity for ideas to emerge from outside of development plans and the traditional hierarchy unless your role description includes crazy future stuff.

Objective

There's more than one way of building a better, bigger brain for innovation. It's good to understand the purpose of building a bigger brain. It's a mistake to believe that any single approach will be the best match for all situations or for all organisations. The best solution is the one that works best.

Bottom up builds a bigger brain by getting more people involved who are lower down in the traditional hierarchy. There are front-line employees who are well placed to find problem-insights and be motivated to find solutions. There are people outside large companies who can share and experiment with ideas and increase the peer-to-peer thinking power applied to solving problems.

Top down is organised to make real the ideas of those at the top of the hierarchy. The advantage can be that roles and direction are unambiguous – with a powerful minority responsible for innovation. The disadvantage is that ideas are not challenged and cannot be easily improved by those without power. Everyone may be expected to simply obey and leave their imaginations at home.

Closed innovation has organisations trying to generate and develop their own ideas. There is often little interest in ideas from outside the formal R&D function. The group wants to own the intellectual property and directs its efforts to solutions that are custom designed to fit its priorities, markets and existing way of doing business.

Open innovation is about finding ideas and solutions from anywhere. The idea is judged on its merits and potential rather than on its origins. There is deliberate focus on building networks of innovation outside the formal organisation. The group shares intellectual property and reuses off-the-shelf innovations. It benefits from the results of mass experimentation. It has access to creativity outside of the confines, bias, politics, point of view and resource limits of the formal organisation.

	Closed innovation	Open innovation
Bottom-up	Our people can understand and solve problems better than outsiders. We want to involve people at all levels because it inspires faster cycles from insight to innovation. We bet on close internal connections rather than depend on external ideas. We own and control processes, ideas and results.	Ideas need to have idea sex. The more variety there is, the more likely we are to find something really worthwhile. The more our ideas are tested by outside eyes, the more they will be improved. We want people at all levels, insights from all angles. We will share, swap, borrow, copy, giveaway and blend.
Top-down	All the smart people are at the top of the hierarchy. The ideas we need to adapt and thrive are kept in formal processes. We don't see how anyone outside of our elite could have anything much to contribute. We don't expect threats from unexpected competition. Employees and partners exist to do what we imagine.	Our elite smart people should be talking to other elite smart people. We are willing to share and partner. We can work with other senior teams to figure out business models for combined innovations. We can swap ideas and license intellectual property. We can benefit from other ideas that work. This is peer-to-peer elitism.

Context

First, consider the flow of ideas around your objectives. Then you can figure out who, and how many, brains are involved in the problem-solving process. Go over the origin of ideas that have contributed the most. Think about how to improve your networks for innovation (see page 236). Give serious thought to how to grow the amount of brainpower engaged in nurturing new ideas.

Second, think about your beliefs about the sources of practical creativity. If you believe in the power of many brains you're going to want to harness more under-appreciated intelligence. If you believe in the power of unusual intellects, you'll want to increase the diversity of minds. If you think of innovation as a game for elite experts, you'll still want to recruit and develop their know-how.

Challenge

The best kind of collective brain for innovation depends on your way of thinking about creativity. Timing will also make a difference and the stage that your idea has already reached. There are extremes in each of these positions. You can have ultra-open and hyper-bottom-up. You can choose to be one innovator in a garage locked up with your work. Or any other combination that works.

Building a better collective brain isn't just about involving *more* people. It can also be about developing the creative skills of people who become involved. You can offer coaching to people outside of the creative elite so that they can be blended into the creative mechanism. People can be invited in by degrees to avoid overwhelming anyone or anything. The brain can evolve.

Amazon claims every team is tasked with innovation. Apple encourages head-office engineers to find competitive solutions to problems defined by top-table brains. Samsung enlarges its innovation brain through a global search for extraordinary creativity in partner companies and universities, while also training people at many levels in creative problem-solving. Nokia got carried away and split effort between three or four mutually destructive brains who never really finished anything.

You have to increase (and improve) connections between people to build a bigger (better) brain. Some of these connections are personal relationships that go beyond the constraints of the organisational chart. People that play together stay creative together. Some connections are about personal affinity with the work or the results of the work. Purpose pulls people together.

There are practical considerations to enlarging the brain beyond the organisation's boundaries. If you're going to share ideas without legal protection those ideas could be borrowed, copied or stolen. One flexible approach is to have simple legal layers that can kick in at various stages of collaboration outside and inside the company. Done right it can reassure everyone involved.

The bigger brain approach is pragmatic. You can't know everything. You can't have all the best ideas or follow every trend. When you plug in the brains of more and more people you'll have new choices because you can't *do* every idea that will be created. One approach is to give people authority to use ideas to improve their own work. You can also provide resources to help them commercialise ideas.

But the bigger brain approach is meant to get you to winning innovation so, as an innovator, you will still have to make decisions. Ideas need to be combined even when some people lose control of their creative babies. Some ideas won't work for you. Other ideas won't work for the next thousand years. It helps if more people can understand the flow of ideas and the shape of innovation, so that they can self-edit in useful ways. This is also part of the evolution of the bigger, better brain.

Success

You'll know that you're building a bigger brain when new ideas start coming from new people. Your approach to innovation is more open. You'll know you've got a better collective brain when more of those ideas become useful innovations. The boundaries between the organisation and the rest of the world do not get in the way of good ideas coming in or good innovations getting out. People are connected around the problems to be solved rather than their seniority or job description.

Innovators will be developed from inside and outside so that the innovation process is adventurous, pragmatic and self-perpetuating. Innovators get what they need so that they can gain the skills necessary to prototype, explore, refine and launch new ideas into the world. Everyone gets better at knowing how to encourage individual exploration and mass experimentation.

Innovator's measure of success

→ You have a way of measuring the flow and direction of new ideas.

→ You encourage interdependent problem-solving at all levels inside and outside the organisation.

→ Your people understand the importance of innovation and the life cycle of ideas.

→ Time for exploration is made part of business-as-usual with new ideas continually brought into the organisation.

→ Communities of ideas emerge and get resources around needs, situations and dreams.

Pitfalls

Despite the checklists on this page, building a bigger brain is not a checklist exercise. You will not be well served by shallow attempts to involve more people. It is not enough to pay for one-way internal communications or glossy marketing campaigns to existing customers. It's too easy to put the effort into the superficial elements rather than the deep extension of the innovation process. You can also weaken existing sources of innovation if you expect instant something-for-nothing creativity.

Innovator's checklist

■ Reward new ideas by encouraging people to make those ideas work. Share more of the benefits from successful new ideas with the people who share their insights.

■ Ensure your innovation process is discussed as part of your training, induction and coaching. Make sure that people understand what drives your innovation imperative and its

challenges. Encourage open discussion about how to improve
and adapt priorities.

■ Bring your people to new ideas. Create a show-and-tell meeting
where new information, scientific principles, products, books
and stories can be shared.

■ Get people connected. Find ways that people can connect.
Help them to establish connections around real-world interests,
problems, dissatisfactions and desired futures.

■ Make people more useful to each other. Give people the
experience of working together in communities of ideas, across
boundaries, with mutual respect and productive outcomes.

■ Assess the evolution of your bigger brain. Think about how well
(or badly) the way you think together is helping you adapting.
Use the tools in this book to improve further.

Related ideas

Building a bigger brain is a way of reducing uncertainty around
innovation efforts because it increases knowledge about the usage
environment, user values and customer decisions (see page 200).
In a similar way, you can gain deeper understanding of design
features that will increase likely adoption of the innovation (see
page 216). Developing the ability of power users to participate
fully in the development process is an amazingly powerful way
of putting highly motivated, naturally talented innovators to
work. This can be further helped by teaching innovation skills
(see page 147).

One more thing

Coloplast, an international medical company with over 7,000
workers, started with a Danish nurse who created an ostomy
bag with an adhesive ring to avoid leakages, so allowing her
sister to leave the house without embarrassment. The company
continues to collaborate with customers. It co-designs products

by increasing understanding of 'intimate health'. The company sponsors idea-sharing communities, user-feedback panels and competitions for new ideas. Tools help users to submit drawings of new designs. Very Innovative Persons (VIPs) are sent proto-typing kits. Coloplast believes in involving people's intelligence and experiences inside and outside the organisation for mutually beneficial innovation.

Do this now!

Start with 10 minutes a week reaching out to people who can be part of a bigger creative brain

Speak openly about new ideas. Stick up hand-drawn quotes. Place adhesive note thoughts on the mirrors in the washrooms. Rip out news clippings that inspire (or annoy) you on the coffee machine. Follow @maxmckeown on Twitter and print out individual tweets to provoke new thoughts and conversations. Share important ideas in articles or books. Find your partners-in-creativity.

Organising people for innovation

Innovation involves a natural tension between chaos and order. If too many new ideas are followed then nothing ever gets finished. If too many old rules are followed then nothing ever gets improved. The challenge is figuring out when (and how) to encourage more ideas, react to new ideas and when to focus people on working together in organised, effective ways.

**Frequency – Use to understand. Refer back to occasionally.
Key participants – Leaders. Anyone who wants to lead.
Innovation rating:******

They should have been building software for their employer. Instead, 15 French programmers asked some very ambitious why and why not questions. Over the next three years, they secretly invested spare time *and* company time building their own vision of 3D design software. When the founder of the aviation company they worked for discovered their secret, he could have shut down the project.

As an inventor himself, he immediately recognised the potential and helped the group spin off a new company – that also bore his name – Dassault Systèmes. The company seeks to blur the lines between digital and physical worlds to help collaborative design, prototyping and production. Its innovation has created a whole new approach. Virtual reality labs are merging with 3D printing to increase the effectiveness and speed of innovation. They are all unashamedly passionate about ideas.

Objective

All new ideas need other people, but there is a cost to organising. It takes time to figure out who does what when. You have to deal with politics, personalities and processes. People can be obstinate, weird, unreliable and annoying. People work together around problems, situations, opportunities and tasks but working with others tends to bring rules, forms, charts and meetings.

There is a cost to doing new things. People can't depend on past experience so they have to consciously think about what has to happen. New ideas offer advantages but those advantages are uncertain. Even if the advantages exist, it may take a lot of time to learn to be efficient again. Effective ways of using (and selling) the new idea have to be discovered, developed and learned.

As a smart innovator, you look at the costs and benefits of people working together. You should recognise that there are different ways of organising people for innovation. As a result, you can choose between the various ways that people work together. You can find approaches for people working together that help generate new ideas and then make them useful – and successful.

Context

People can be organised on a non-permanent basis

They can be organised around a particular (temporary) innovation objective. These teams vary according to who is formally in authority, the level of commitment of team members and how independent the team is from the business-as-usual mentality.

Functional teams	Lightweight teams	Heavyweight teams	Autonomous
Resource authority, assignment of team members and approach stays with the functional power structure and processes.	Coordination committee with light project management and with work done back in the various functions.	Senior full-time project managers organise for project purpose that guides work done in functions.	Members of the team are transferred outside of their functions – with their own project management and processes.

Each team design offers different advantages and disadvantages. Functional teams can be over-standardised, because they follow functional processes, and under-focused, because they follow functional priorities. Lightweight teams have better coordination but no real authority, while heavyweight teams have authority but still do not focus only on the innovation.

People can be organised on a more permanent basis

Organisations vary according to how well they explore new ideas, their effectiveness in exploiting existing ideas and direction of idea flow. Some argue more radical innovation is best done by autonomous groups with organic cultures while the main organisation with a more mechanistic culture focuses on efficiency. Others argue for ambidextrous organisations that can explore and exploit with the same people behaving in different ways.

Mechanistic	Organic	Ambidextrous
Top-down hierarchy decides and prioritises tasks for people with specialities.	Collaborative process for decisions and priorities for teams by teams.	Approach to decisions and priorities depend on context.
Focuses on efficiency and exploitation of existing ideas	Focuses on effectiveness and exploration of new ideas.	Focused on exploration *and* exploitation.
New ideas flow down between roles and rules.	New ideas flow between ambition and ability.	New ideas co-exist and co-evolve with existing ideas.
Status based on power and resources.	Status based on reputation and talent.	Status based on contribution towards new and future goals.

Each organisation design offers advantages and disadvantages to innovation. **Mechanistic hierarchies** can get in the way of innovation by discouraging the cross-pollination of ideas and insights. Yet the same hierarchy can also be paired with continual improvement processes to drive relentlessly towards cumulative breakthroughs – thereby making ethereal ideas solid and successful.

The **organic organisation** can be powerfully focused on exploring new ideas but suffers from novelty overload. Many different new ideas fight for attention, time and resources. New ideas can stall and stagnate because every decision is complex and painful. The reputations of innovation gods can block contributions from lesser mortals. Too much exploration can be bad for organisational health.

Ambidextrous organisations attempt a powerful mix of exploration and exploitation. A dual system allows a blend of priorities and benefits. Some people focus on getting the most out of ideas by using them in proven ways and making continual improvements. Other people work in teams to focus on creating new ideas and experimenting until those ideas can contribute on a day-to-day basis.

People can be organised on a networked basis

Organisations vary in how effectively they recognise the importance of networks for the success of innovation. Ideas flow between people. New ideas emerge from individual brains that are connected to other ideas and individuals. Networks come in different shapes, styles and sizes. There are open, closed, weak and strong networks. There are also formal, informal, fluid and rigid networks. Every idea and person interacts with multiple networks.

	Closed	Open
Weak	*Many weak connections* between many different people across *rigid boundaries* inside and outside the formal organisation	*Many weak connections* between many different people across *fluid boundaries* inside and outside the formal organisation
Strong	*Few strong connections* between small numbers of people across *rigid boundaries* inside and outside the formal organisation	*Few strong connections* between small numbers of people across *fluid boundaries* inside and outside the formal organisation

Effective innovation comes from the creative use of many different types of network. Strong connections help with smooth working relations, emotional commitment and deep shared knowledge from creative partnership. Weak connections increase the chance you'll share information and perspectives that are old to you but new to someone else.

Challenge

Culture matters as much (or more) than structure. You can choose any formal team, organisational or network design but still be dependent on the informal ways that people interact. If the climate of your artfully autonomous team is still deeply dependent there will be very little thinking outside of its typical functional constraints. You can take a team member out of the specialism but struggle to take the specialist mindset out of the team member.

It's important to remember the *purpose* behind any particular way of organising people. If you want more innovation in general then the success of the group design should be judged on general innovation. If you have specific problems then the group needs to be measured on specific creative solutions. The stage of the innovation journey also changes the blend of people and process that are likely to be useful. Exploration of new ideas is quite different to exploitation of those new ideas.

Smart innovators deliberately encourage networks to emerge around new ideas *and* around the existing formal organisation. They develop the capability of individuals to choose when to explore or exploit depending on what seems most valuable in any particular situation or context.

Success

You're getting better at organising people for innovation when the style and substance of organisation is a good match to the kind of innovation that you want. Instead of relying on top-down hierarchies and the talent of a few individuals to get things done, you are working towards a powerful combination of flexible teams, open networks and ambidextrous individuals.

Being a smart innovator is often about managing paradox and tension. Your approach to organising people for innovation, embraces the tension between exploring (finding, generating, discovering) and exploiting (developing, producing, using) new ideas. People at all levels are encouraged to take a full part in adapting to situations now and in the future. Adaptation is a mass participation activity.

Innovator's measure of success

➤ You understand the range of options for organising people for innovation.

➤ Differences between shallow form and deep function for innovation are recognised.

➤ Along the innovation journey, you can flip between exploration and exploitation.

➤ People inside and outside the organisation contribute to (ambidextrous) adaptation.

Pitfalls

Structure can be a major distraction from innovation. Many leaders get trapped in perpetual reorganisations that fail to help increase creativity or the effective use of new ideas. It's tempting to believe that there is one perfect organisational design that works for all circumstances. People can slavishly follow the shallow templates of other organisations rather than finding deep ways of working together that are original and effective. It's very easy to waste the natural differences between your people and other organisations. The danger is in putting structure before culture.

Innovator's checklist

■ Consider the flow of new ideas. How does the way people are organised help (or hinder) new ideas to be created? Does the organisation speed up (or slow down) the sharing of new ideas? Are there new idea bottle-necks? Which parts of the organisation are blamed for blocking new ideas? Does the organisation encourage exploration or exploitation?

■ Use the notion of convergence and divergence to better understand how the best way of organising for innovation will ebb and flow (see page 172). Consider the shape of the innovation journey (see page 185) related to different kinds of teams and networks. Think about how ideas build cumulatively through people into innovation (see page 189).

■ Think about the situation inside and outside your group. If uncertainty and competition is high then you'll need more exploration than exploitation. Too much exploration is damaging but organisations are more likely to not do enough than too much. Talk with your people about the costs, benefits and purpose of the various teams, structures and networks.

Related ideas

Some exploration will lead to new opportunities but all exploration can lead to new capacity. This includes the *absorptive capacity* to benefit from new ideas. People need to be able to understand the new idea and have the ability, time and resources to use it effectively. For successful adaptation, you need internal change that matches external change in terms of speed and shape. This only happens if your organisation has the *dynamic capability* to assess and use new ideas. This means that you need to learn from direct experience and advances of competitors and innovators *as they happen* rather than at the start or end of specific projects or planning cycles.

One more thing

Horrible Histories was the first children's television show to win the best sketch at the British Comedy Awards. It was also one of the very few children's programmes to gain a cross-over audience.

Based on a series of popular books of the same name (that sold 20 million copies) the idea was originally pitched along very generic lines but the BBC wanted it to be something much bolder. A chance meeting with a very successful comedy director led to the idea of a sketch show format.

Award-winning comedy actors and writers were recruited. They adapted the ideas sitting around a table with the author and a historical adviser. They read the books in a circle until someone thought of a way to portray a historical event as a comedy sketch which would then be written. They could naturally go further than most competing ideas because they figured out how to combine the best of the original idea with traditions of a very different set of ideas. This blending was innovation genius.

Do this now!

Spend 10 minutes finding out whether anyone has done something similar to your new idea ☐

Use a search engine to look for similar ideas. Find people who have experience with the problem you're trying to solve. They can help you figure out whether there is already a solution. You don't want to waste valuable time recreating something no better than existing solutions. If you find something similar then it provides a benchmark or a starting point for your breakthrough (see page 245 on innovator's clubs).

Creating a powerful innovation culture

Innovation is all about extending what is possible. Before your new insight, the future you desired was impossible or unlikely. After your new idea, something that was hard becomes easy. Leading innovation is about inspiring people to see (and want) better futures. Getting people to do what they love is the most effective way of inspiring creativity and commitment to that better future.

Frequency: Business-as-usual, frequent recommitment.
Key participants: Leadership team, everyone.
Strategy rating:****

Kweichow Moutai started as a producer of traditional liquor – Moutai – from Southwest China. The drink it produces has a distinctive soy-sauce fragrance and the company has a distinctive culture of innovation. The culture of innovation developed from a 2,000-year creative brewing tradition into what is now termed the Three Concepts of Moutai.

Green Moutai is about ensuring that every supplier and part of the production process is both organic and protective of the environment. *Hi-Tech Moutai* reflects the continued drive to use science to better understand the unique attributes of the company's alcohol and to improve it. *Cultural Moutai* involves inspiring people to believe in the long-term value of the company's purpose.

These traditions of creativity have led Moutai to invest in many different aspects of R&D. This includes working with universities to establish the chromatographic fingerprint of its alcohol and produce patentable technologies. This has improved quality control, the marketing of the product and identification of fake products. The combination also inspires employees to keep innovating.

Objective

New ideas are created and used by people. Innovation culture is how we describe how – effectively or ineffectively – people work together to create and use new ideas.

Culture is the sum of the values, beliefs and assumptions of human groups. Culture is about the personality and behaviour of a social group. It is all the different forces that shape what groups are likely to do next. These flavours, traditions, norms and attitudes distinguish one group from another. The culture of your organisation shapes the way people create, think and solve problems.

Idea-toxic	Idea-wasteful	Idea-friendly	Idea-hungry
Creativity is not welcome or rewarded. There is indifference, apathy or fear about new ideas and change.	New ideas and insights are treated casually and mismanaged. Creativity is seen as a threat to productivity.	Creativity is welcomed since new ideas are valued. New ideas may get introduced and reviewed by hierarchy.	People seek new ideas. They make the world better with radical improvement beyond existing limits.

Some parts of any culture will encourage innovation while other parts will discourage innovation. The idea-toxic culture hides from newness and behind the defences of tradition, rank and inertia while the idea-hungry culture celebrates both novelty and its ability to transform the world. The highly innovative group also tends to be highly attached to a shared identity as a creative force.

In an idea-hungry culture, real-world experience with experimentation prepares individuals to thrive amid sporadic, unpredictable, externally linked, waves of innovation.

Involvement in hunting ideas and solutions conditions creative muscles to cope with uncertainties, fast change and slow pay-off. There is a collective awareness of what it takes and willingness to do what it takes.

Context

No culture is a vacuum. Everyone comes into your group from another group. Every organisational culture lives alongside regional, professional or national cultures.

When you want to encourage creativity, you have to contend with anti-creative attitudes and unhelpful assumptions picked up from other places and learned from other experiences. Too many efforts to increase innovation ignore the way that people think and feel in their day-to-day work.

Too few innovation projects empower daily working lives with the result that too few people gain working knowledge, and belief, in their ability to improve and change their own organisations. If you don't allow people to change what matters most to them, why would they ever engage their precious creativity in solving problems that matter to you?

It helps to signal how things are different. Put the power to change the organisation in the hands of those people you expect to be creative. Help people experience the lives, worries, headaches and passions of their colleagues and customers. Innovation cultures feel different. There is a happy excess of imagination, daring, initiative and play. Creative experience feeds creative behaviour.

Challenge

The first challenge is to encourage creative behaviour that leads to successful innovation. The second challenge is to develop a tradition of creative behaviour that keeps leading to more and more successful innovation. Both of these challenges are about the climate and conditions that encourage – or discourage – the effective use of new ideas. They are both about cultural change.

Raising expectation is about higher ambition leading to innovation because it becomes an attractive way – or the only way – of achieving those bigger, bolder goals. Introducing examples of better (products, services, processes and results) prompts desire to achieve better. Understanding how other organisations involve the creativity of people at all levels (frontline, middle, specialist and top) resets assumptions about collaboration. Seeing, feeling, tasting, experiencing real innovation helps.

Increasing experimentation is about learning-by-doing so that innovation is done better and more often because people find innovation easier and more productive. Introducing more people to how real-world innovation is done (science, hypotheses, testing and prototypes) prompts them to try. Getting involved with practical experiments develops innovation skills, habits and thinking styles. Helping people become comfortable playing with the cutting edge and exploring the unknown is the goal.

Lowering barriers is about bringing people and ideas together to make it more likely that ideas combine and people collaborate. Dissolving boundaries between cliques, teams, departments, professions, seating plans and personalities helps find the insights for breakthrough innovation. Making it easier to gain the knowledge, information and resources that innovators need is how you discover new innovation superstars. Mix up the day-to-day. Deliberately open minds and plans.

Innovation is about practical creativity. That's why developing an innovation culture is about developing practical creativity as groups. Try not to get lost in too much corporate talk about adding layers of complication. Encourage experimentation, raise expectations, and lower barriers.

Success

You're succeeding with innovation culture when people are idea hungry. They actively seek out new ideas and know how to nurture them. Everyone is involved with bringing ideas to the group. People reach out beyond tasks to trends, behind projects to purpose. They talk about the possibility and reality of break-throughs. People are connected to each other, to the outside world and to dreams.

New ideas come from every part of the organisation (and beyond). Ideas are understood, prodded, tested, developed and trialled before they are even formally proposed. Every individual understands how to progress bits of insight into something more substantial. People have innovation partners, buddies, mates, pals, friends, conspirators, allies, comrades, playmates, intimates and muses.

People know that every innovation has a sell-by-date. They move between different time frames. They work to make existing ideas work on a day-to-day basis, improve existing ideas for the-next-day and find day-after-tomorrow breakthroughs that can replace the way things are done now. The language of innovation (theory and practice) is the mother tongue – shaping thought and action. You are surrounded by a diversity of makers and thinkers working together to make better futures.

Innovator's measure of success

- Everyone is an innovator.
- Ideas (start to) come from everywhere.
- People (begin to) see impossible as motivational.
- Fluid networks nurture insights and ideas.
- People speak the deep language of innovation.

Pitfalls

It's dangerous to think that innovation culture solves every-thing. You can have an idea-hungry culture and still fail in the real world. People can become overwhelmed by big cultural change programmes imposed top-down as an attempt to increase bottom-up innovation. Bottle-necks of expectation may develop between what is promised and what happens. Traditional hierarchy and habits often reassert themselves as people worry about loss of control or fear of failure. Efforts to improve creativity, initiative and ambition fail because they stay theoretical rather than practical.

Innovator's checklist

▓ Take a look at the existing culture in your organisation. Talk to people about where new ideas emerge. Ask people in different teams and positions about what happens when they have a new idea. How innovative are the ideas that get attention? How many new ideas get implemented? Do people tend to have positive or negative experiences with innovation? Are they hungry for change?

▓ Develop an innovation hub. Have a library of new ideas. Provide open-access learning about how to solve problems creatively. Collect experiences with practical innovation. Provide a home-from-home for incurable radicals, experienced campaigners and curious novices. Offer idea-clinics to show people how to develop their own ideas. Create your own mini-culture.

▓ Inject innovation into the cultural circulatory system. Regular team meetings can be adjusted to encourage and develop new ideas. Add a creative show-and-tell where different people share insights, technology, trends or problems. Ensure reward and recognition system includes innovation. Redesign training to teach innovation. Add diversity to recruitment and role descriptions. Encourage playfulness and improvement everywhere.

▓ Democratise sophistication. Pin up diagrams like the innovation pyramid (see page 150) on walls. Make them poster-size. Get everyone involved in discussions about concepts that explain how innovation works.

Related ideas

Edgar Schein, MIT psychologist, introduced a three-level model of culture. *Artefacts* are visible parts including physical (buildings, design, clothing, objects) and behavioural (jokes, language, posture, actions). *Values* are what groups say publicly about beliefs and rules for behaviour. *Shared Basic Assumptions* are about invisible, taken-for-granted viewpoints and priorities. The way people work with new ideas in a culture depends on artefacts, values and assumptions. All three can change.

One more thing

One of the first 3D printing pioneers was Charles Hull. He was investigating one thing (resins that could be cured with ultraviolet light) when the insight into another thing happened. Frustrated with the time taken to make prototype plastic parts, he figured out a way of combining photochemistry, lasers, scanning optics and software to 'print' 3D objects by building up a pattern layer by layer. He built it himself with lab time donated by his employer before turning it into a commercial product. Thirty years later and 3D printers have been used to print cars, planes, robots and even replacement organs. A post-industrial revolution is emerging from this 3D community.

Do this now!

Devote 60 minutes a week to some kind of creativity get-together. Start this month ☐

Start informal. Grow by iterations of enthusiasm – and results. Gather together in a bar, coffee house, canteen, restaurant, art gallery, park or sports ground. Innovation groups. Play. Discover. Buzz sessions. All-night problem festivals. Build the credibility of the process and the people involved. Make innovation stars and creativity heroes. Start with one or two people. Then recruit a handful, by recommendation or word of mouth. Take photos. Don't create false urgency. Simply enjoy.

Motivating innovators

Beautiful ideas inspire the future actions of innovators. Big ideas shape the expectations of generations. Successful innovations influence the behaviour of people living in each age. There is nothing as powerful as a provocative idea. To shape a better future you need better ideas.

Frequency – Use to motivate your team. And to design rewards and work.
Key participants – Leaders. HR. Talent. Those who want to understand motivation.
Innovation rating:****

'To boldly go where no man has gone before' was a line used in the second pilot of *Star Trek*. Its origins are not clear but similar phrases were used by Captain Cook on his voyages. It was used back in 1958 in proposals to gain US public support for a space exploration to compete with Sputnik. Later, US President Kennedy challenged his country to make a moon landing within a decade. He argued that the goal was worthwhile 'not because it was easy, but because it was hard'.

The USA was not the first. People around the world were inspired by the challenge of space travel. The fiction of Jules Verne and H.G. Wells captured the imagination of scientists who wanted to make fantasy real. Breakthroughs driven by scientific curiosity in one country were used by scientists in other nations to motivate government decisions and funding.

The Von Braun team, transplanted from Germany to the USA, proposed (crazy) space stations and moon bases. The Korolev team, innovating despite interference from Five-Year Plans, got animals, people and satellites in space first. Its successes prompted multi-billion dollar investments in NASA that led to the moon, a civilian space industry and missions to Mars for China and India.

Objective

Human history is all about the power of ideas to motivate actions. Our actions are guided by ideas, and changes in our behaviour are shaped by changes to those ideas. Different people respond to different ideas. Some are driven by the impossible dream, others are engaged with the eminently sensible next logical improvement.

Challenge motivators are about trying to make something new work. The satisfaction of fixing something that's broken or transcending previous limitations. Making history is worth making an effort, particularly efforts that are discretionary. The more complex the problem, the more dedication is needed to figure out a better solution. This dedication is provoked by challenge.

Hindrance demotivators are what stop you getting on with work that matters. Politics in the office. Processes that seem nonsensical or unnecessary. Confusion over roles. Missing resources that you need (or think you need) to accomplish what you consider as the real objective. These hindrances tend to irritate, depress, annoy and generally cause unproductive, unhelpful moods and behaviours.

Prosocial motivators are what happens when you focus on finding new ideas to help other people. It could be about caring for other people, because you think helping others is ethically right, or to make you feel good. Prosocial motivation adds to creativity because it focuses attention on outcomes (rather than just tasks) and on better futures (rather than just present enjoyment).

It can be creatively motivating to try and achieve something remarkable against time pressure. Or to have lots of different kinds of problems to solve. But it is usually demotivating if you don't believe you will ever find creative solutions or if you don't believe your work makes a difference to anyone. People need the motivation to acquire the skills and knowledge to innovate and they need the motivation to work through the innovation process until they make ideas useful.

Context

Innovation can feel like hard work with an uncertain outcome. The hard work involved in innovation is only done when people feel sufficiently motivated. Some leaders assume that only senior people are responsible for creativity so don't worry about motivating people through the organisation. They may believe people are only motivated by external rewards. This limited view leads them to ignore more powerful sources of motivation and the people who are more valuable sources of innovation.

In the real world, your enjoyment in *doing* a particular creative task may be relatively unimportant compared to your expectations for the ultimate purpose or outcome of your creative work. Your motivation for innovating will also be affected by beliefs about the likelihood of success. If people feel they will (probably) fail they are less likely to invest the necessary levels of effort. This is particularly true if people don't even value the learning that comes from trying something new.

Life in organisations can be very efficient at demotivating effort – particularly the kind of discretionary effort that innovation needs. They can slow you down and frustrate your best efforts. They can separate you from ideas you love, problems you care about or that sense of progress that makes the innovation pain worthwhile. Fragmentation can also stop you learning enough about the whole process to leave you feeling more confident that success is more likely as you gain experience.

Challenge

The challenge is to create a self-perpetuating cycle of motivation. You want to increase motivational beliefs that increase creativity success that in turn increases motivation to innovate. One way to establish a motivational cycle is getting people involved in the complete innovation life cycles. The more people practise innovation, the more confident they feel in their ability to innovate.

The next step is to link what people care about with their efforts to innovate. Some people love doing particular parts of the work. Love of doing a task can be transformed into the kind of intrinsic motivation to improve the way that task is done. This works because people are more open to experience when doing what they enjoy and because they do the task enough times to gain real insights into the limits of the way the job is done. They are motivated *and* knowledgeable.

Some people love making a difference in the lives of others. Thinking about the needs of others is very motivating beyond enjoying particular kinds of work – it motivates people to think about how innovation can improve overall outcomes for other people. It moves focus from the short-term to the long-term future. This helps because people think big in ways that require innovation – and think far enough into the future to encourage the impatience and patience necessary for breakthroughs.

Success

You will be getting better at motivating innovators when you understand the cycles of motivation and demotivation. You can see some of your own motivations to innovate and deliberately challenge your perspective to find more of the motivations that help you do your best creative work. You find what you love doing but – more importantly – you find desirable outcomes that keep you going.

Progress has been in reducing the demotivators of creativity. External pressures – including deadlines – are used intelligently to provide creative urgency rather than overwhelming creative efforts with worry. Changes to deadlines and criteria are carefully managed to sustain the sense of progress that is important to levels of motivational energy.

Innovator's measure of success

→ You understand different kinds of innovation motivators and demotivators.

→ People are matched to their most powerful motivators.

→ Making the world better for others is used to increase future focus.

→ People become more confident about their ability to innovate.

→ Urgency is based on real opportunities rather than false pressure.

Pitfalls

The relationship between motivation and innovation is not simple. It's unwise to assume that time pressure, external rewards, impossible goals or criticism are bad – or good. The same approach to motivation will not work for all circumstances, for all stages of innovation or for all personalities. You could fail to notice how external support shapes whether pressures are viewed as threat or opportunity. You might fail to motivate the specific kind of creativity behaviour that is needed.

Innovator's checklist

■ Identify the worst demotivators. Who are the most damaging demotivators? What are the most demotivating behaviours? How can you banish hindrance demotivators from working lives? Where are the blockers stopping people from doing their work? When does time pressure start to overwhelm your people? Can you transform demotivational appraisals and rewards?

■ Explore the most powerful motivators. Are people doing work they intrinsically love? How can you find out more about the learning outcomes that motivate people? Where is the sense of progress each day? How can practical innovation support be provided? How can you introduce motivational collaboration? How about doing work people find important?

Related ideas

Professor Teresa Amabile, HBS organisational psychologist, is famous for arguing that intrinsic motivation is essential to individual creativity while extrinsic rewards can be damaging. She has also found that one of the most powerful motivators in the workplace is our sense of progression. People want to feel that their effort has moved their work forward. When managers unilaterally change goals, are indecisive or delay necessary resources – they reduce motivation necessary to creativity.

One more thing

After Polaroid – the company – passed away into bankruptcy Polaroid – the concept – was reborn. Creativity is flowing again around the idea of instant prints. Enthusiasts acted to bring back traditional Polaroid film by building a factory in Poland they called Project Impossible. Entrepreneurs launched a chain of Polaroid Fotobars with Fototenders to turn your best pictures into artwork. There's an Android Smart camera with interchangeable lens. A digital camera with built-in printer. And an iPhone app. Polaroid's new motto is: 75 Years Young. What will happen next?

Do this now!

Invest 30 minutes with your team discussing pro-innovation and anti-innovation cultures

Use plastic bricks or modelling clay to build different kinds of new idea cultures. Get half the team to build an anti-innovation organisation for killing new ideas. Get half the team to build a pro-innovation organisation to look after new ideas. Identify three differences between the pro-innovation and anti-innovation approaches. Discuss how to improve how new ideas are treated.

three

Creating innovation

'Controversy is part of the nature of art and creativity.'
Yoko Ono

As an innovator, you are trying to move from the existing situation to something better. Moving to something better is only possible if you can travel successfully along the innovation curve.

You can use the power of creative rebels to go beyond existing constraints. The spirit of creative rebellion is willing to pay the price for new knowledge, new methods and new skills.

The creative maverick is ready to sacrifice short-term gains for longer-term gains for the good of other people. This willingness to abandon the old comforts for new wonders leads to breakthrough innovations.

One powerful way of inspiring innovation is to focus attention on usefulness – now and in the future. Over time, increases in any particular way of doing things will diminish.

You can make small improvements but big improvements are no longer possible. The only way of making big new improvements is to jump onto a new innovation curve by investing creativity in new possibilities.

If ideas are judged for newness *and* potential usefulness, the path from insight to innovation becomes more effective. By engaging with controversy, the motivations of those who want to solve problems and those who want to make a difference are brought together.

The role of investors, managers, sponsors and partners becomes clearer because they are encouraging work towards an agreed overall objective. Everyone can measure progress along the innovation curve towards new levels of usefulness.

Using the power of (creative) rebels

If traditional doesn't work, traditions won't do. Habits make it difficult for people to see how anything could be different. Innovation needs rebellion. You can free your inner rebel by feeding both your curiosity and willingness to question. Smart leaders of innovation seek to engage the intellectual freedom of mavericks. They value those who reject limitations of what is possible.

Frequency – Once. And then whenever creative spirits cause problems.
Key participants – First you. Then, everyone.
Innovation rating –****

When a patent clerk, Genrich Altshuller, proposed improvements to how the USSR innovated, he was imprisoned as an enemy of the state. He survived interrogation and labour camps through his quick-witted problem-solving. Later, his ideas about practical creativity spread into Russian universities where idea scouts brought the techniques back to Samsung in Seoul. The rebel mind persecuted under one system became a powerful source of innovation in an idea-hungry culture.

When a second patent clerk, Albert Einstein, proposed radical new theories about space and time, he shared his thought experiments with friends. Yet his brilliant rebelliousness was rejected by the idea-toxic culture of Nazi Germany. They burned his books and put a price upon his head. Many such beautiful minds brutally discarded by narrow prejudice were embraced warmly in the USA.

Objective

Innovation is deviance which means that the rebellious personality is a natural resource for practical creativity. As an innovator, you need to reject the old to establish a new (better) status quo. One of the most powerful sources of newness is the rebel (or maverick) mind.

You need to plug into the anti-obvious power of the rebel. Or you want those opposing minds to plug into your purpose, to solve your problem, to reimagine your process.

Outsider brains find conformity painful. Their alternative viewpoint can easily lead them to step back from the crowd – so far back that the crowd forget they exist. Or they can disagree so frequently that the group steps away from the innovation odour of their inconvenient opinions. The dissenter may be isolated or ignored, discredited, persecuted, punished or pressurised to quit or conform.

It's worth asking:

- Where are your creative rebels and mavericks?
- How effectively are your rebel minds being utilised?
- Is rebellion (or idea diversity) increasing or decreasing?
- Where are the existing boundaries of tradition or know-how?

Groups are defined by them and us. There are rules for membership. Rules can be formal, informal, spoken, unspoken, known or unknown. Even small differences can decide who fits and who doesn't. Anyone who doesn't fit is thrown out. Anything that doesn't fit is chopped off. Even the most creative beginnings can lead to anti-creative ends, unless you develop and defend new traditions of anti-tradition.

Context

Many organisations unintentionally reduce innovation through efforts to increase consistency. There are formal job advertisements with essential and desirable attributes. These are added to formal job descriptions within the formal hierarchy. And let's not forget formal review processes, with managers sorting people into categories based on formal performance criteria.

To complete the sameness filter, some systems fire those who are at the bottom of the rankings. Unfortunately, despite good intentions, this is a process that can damage the ability of the group to adapt to new conditions *or* introduce new ideas that can transform the future.

One problem is that people with new ideas can pay a personal price for sharing them. And they may be offered no encouragement to defend, develop or distribute their new ideas. The group likes stability even if stability is often an illusion. Colleagues may minimise, attack or deny opinions just because they are different. People may fight against new ideas because they feel criticised, feel their way of life is threatened, or feel stupid.

Innovation needs openness to new ideas but the people who desperately need openness are also the least likely to embrace those ideas that can save them. You need people who defy convention because it helps create space for new ideas and learning throughout your group, team or society. You also need enough people to work within convention to make any new ideas work.

Challenge

The secret is to influence the climate of practical creativity. You want people to care about the success of the overall purpose of the group. You often need people to be willing to challenge rules while working within those rules. Understanding four behavioural types is helpful in making this work.

Soldiers keep the rules. They conform to conventions. They follow, obey and are willing supporters of the success of the organisation. They share the objectives of the group and they want the group to be successful. They may try to suppress different views and reject those who share them.

Conformers also keep the rules. They want to fit in. They dress, speak and act in ways that are necessary to be seen as one of the group. But they don't share the objectives of the group or necessarily want the group to be successful. They may obey even when the rules make no sense.

Rebels break the rules. They actively reject some – or all – of the group's traditions. They may think, dress and act in deliberate defiance of the way things are usually done. They have also rejected the objectives of the group and are not interested in whether the group succeeds. They are easy to spot.

Mavericks also break rules. They challenge conventions and intentionally break with traditions. But they are interested in the overall well-being of the group. They often argue, suggest and disobey in what they see as the best interests of the group. They are working and thinking for the greater good.

These behaviours are not fixed. Good soldiers can learn to challenge traditions when challenging traditions is seen as something that is good for the group. Unhappy mavericks can become rebels if they stop believing in the purpose of the group. The smart leader of innovation can try to shape a climate of adaptability that responds to the needs of the moment with conformity or creativity.

Success

You've got an effective blend of agreement, disagreement, obedience and disobedience. There's enough agreement to get work finished. There's enough disagreement to test assumptions and find better alternatives. Lots of different kinds of people and viewpoints help to make new ideas work in the real world. You have increased your understanding of how the dynamics of difference interact and you are able to better change the climate of creativity to engage the different talent you need.

You recruit diversity. Your process for getting people involved is deliberately designed to attract difference. Job descriptions include new ideas and asking tough new questions. People understand the dangers of conformity – and, as a result, they value the protection offered by rebellious ambition. There is a hunger for new perspectives. You can move between order and chaos as needed.

Innovator's measure of success

➤ You have a way of deliberately recruiting difference.

➤ You recognise rebel, soldier, conformer and maverick behaviours.

➤ Everyone knows business-as-usual will eventually fail.

➤ Your assessment, reward and planning processes are built to encourage effective interplay between the different behaviours and viewpoints.

➤ Meetings and interactions between people encourage active blending of viewpoints.

➤ Outsiders are hired to challenge what insiders take for granted.

Pitfalls

Valuing difference is not the same as wanting never-ending disagreement. Some groups are so fragmented that they become dysfunctional. Not all rebellion is born of oppression or helpful insights. Old debates and arguments can become stagnant with no progress on any side. Individuals can offer lazy criticism. Reviews, brainstorms and attempts to find alternatives can become shallow exercises that waste time but are not seriously considered. The dissenting voice becomes a shallow checklist while the maverick is viewed as court jester rather than as an effective provocateur.

Innovator's checklist

■ Assess your existing blend of sameness and difference. Think about the efforts your organisation (or company) make to increase 'consistency' or 'alignment'. Consider how recruitment, review and reward systems may lead to standardised world views.

■ Identify sources of dissent: who is doing any active disagreement? Identify deviance: who is travelling in a different direction? Identify difference: who has different opinions or behaviour? Identify sources of defiance: who is openly standing up against prevailing views?

■ Compare levels of creative diversity in your organisation with those that are more innovative. Look at how organisations that have lost their innovative edge have previously become over-standardised. If you are facing a crisis of standardisation, you may have to respond with an injection of rebelliousness – and look after it so it contributes.

■ Introduce the rebel, maverick, soldier, conformer concepts to your team. Discuss the value of each of them to the success of the group – particularly in shaping a better future. The evidence is that people more easily value diversity when they see how it helps them.

■ Think about the difference between breaking rules and rejecting traditions. Most people find it simpler to deal with those who break rules because it is more straightforward to punish or rehabilitate. Yet open rejection of traditions challenge the beliefs of the group.

■ Help people to share dissenting opinions in ways likely to help innovation. Different (or new) people are valuable but less likely to be accepted. You need a particular blend of novelty and credibility for ideas to change circumstances and change minds.

Related ideas

One way of making difference work for the group is to deliberately introduce constructive conflict (see page 231). In this way, dissenting voices have a more accepted role – while traditional voices are able to play the role of rebel or maverick.

One more thing

Freeing your inner rebel, artist or maverick can be as important as releasing those around you. Justin Bieber, despite criticism, has that impulse to create and share. He seems happier when able to share his creations, regardless of the people who say they hate his music, whether covers of R&B stars or songs he has written. After two albums, he released a series of 10 musical experiments. More personal and less commercial, they were announced each week to his 46 million Twitter followers. According to his manager, sharing directly is part of showing Bieber can play the game differently.

Do this now!

Arrange to have a chat with one of the most creative rebels (or thinkers) you know

Who do you know that dresses, speaks, thinks or acts differently? The director of *The Incredibles*, Brad Bird, asked Pixar to 'give us the black sheep. I want artists who are frustrated. I want the ones who have another way of doing things that nobody's listening to. Give us the guys who are probably heading out the door.' Brad encourages the rebels to prove their theories. Encourage your rebels.

Making new ideas useful

The smart innovator is interested in what new ideas can do. They value the new idea for what it allows them to try and understand. They are driven by how the previously impossible (or difficult) can be made possible (or easy). As an innovator, your work is to make new ideas useful.

Frequency – Always. Continually. It's the heart of innovation.
Key participants – First you. Then, everyone.
Innovation rating – Innovation6

The electric car is an idea but not a new idea. There were electric cars in the 19th century but they didn't prove as successful as the internal combustion engine. Recent efforts to make electric cars popular in the real world require more than an electric engine. They need better questions until the innovation is complete enough to solve enough valuable real-world problems to thrive.

Chetan Maini developed the Reva Electric Car Company in Bangalore as a series of smart questions. His father had asked how a small car could help India. Chetan asked how an affordable compact electric car could contribute to solving urban pollution. The company asked how it could reduce purchase costs and ended up in partnership with rental firms. It asked how it could improve the technology of electric cars and patented breakthrough engine management systems.

Asking better questions is business-as-usual for Reva. Asking how the company could get access to global technology led to the original joint venture with a US company. Asking how it could scale up production helped it give up a controlling interest for investment from Mahindra and Mahindra – one of India's largest manufacturers. The company has now launched the 'Ask Movement' to encourage people inside and outside to ask better questions that will help create real progress.

Objective

Innovators help make new ideas useful. They are not always the originator of the scientific breakthrough – although they can be. Even when they have to make scientific progress their focus is on solving practical problems. The innovator may not win a Nobel Prize but can still change the world.

There is a desire for newness from those who love novelty and those who want to market or sell novelty – although there is a difference between wanting features for advertisements and wanting to tinker with new toys. This difference creates a gap between the two meanings of newness. The gap can cause misunderstanding between the focus of innovation efforts.

There is a desire for usefulness from potential users of the innovation and those who want to make the world better – although there can be a difference between how various people perceive usefulness. This difference creates a gap between various meanings of usefulness. The gap can cause innovators to focus on what they want rather than how others will use the new ideas in practice.

In the absence of anything better, effort is focused on generating lists of new features that may offer very little to the potential user. New features may even make things worse. They may add extra cost or complication that make what you are offering less attractive. This effort can create opportunities for innovators to compete by simplifying or localising what is offered to increase usefulness.

Context

Most people want to know what innovation does for them rather than how it works. People are more interested in using something they perceive as being useful. Not many people want to understand the science or inner-workings of a thing, just how the idea helps them.

There can be a gap between the interests of the inventor (who knows how to build the new idea) and the user (who is meant to use the new idea). Before a new idea is ever made to work, there are thinkers who see the possibilities (decades and millennia into the future) and makers who enjoy the newness and the thrill of understanding. They love the mechanics, the arcane detail and the work.

Because they love the detail and know how to make things work, inventors can live with levels of complication that would be off-putting to most people. They can be so focused on making something work that they forget about making it useful to people who lack their knowledge and interest. They may not care much about beautiful design and ease of use. Their judgement of *net usefulness* is different. They can't see their new idea through the eyes of the rest of the world.

Usability design can help to reduce usage cost but is of limited importance unless total perceived usefulness increases. You have to consider what is valuable to your potential users. You also have to think about what is considered valueless to your potential users because this needs to be reduced (taken away) or presented in new ways that are valuable.

Challenge

For more useful ideas you need better problems. To find – and solve – better problems you'll need better questions. The original insight needs an original question. The new idea needs a new question. More importantly, a new idea needs a complete set of questions to become complete innovation. The challenge is to focus your group on finding a powerful blend of new and useful.

Many discussions about improvement are limited by old assumptions. Many new ideas are rejected because their usefulness is unclear to people who have lower tolerance for newness. The trick is to get everyone focused on the limits of existing approaches and benefits of new approaches, in terms of net usefulness. This will make something you care about easier to do, achieve or experience.

Localising is about making something more useful in a particular situation. You can localise to the needs of a specific person or group of people. You can localise to a language, nation, task or industry. Something can be localised in shallow ways to make usefulness more obvious. Deep localisation reaches into how people think, work or play to improve something significant.

Simplifying is about making the path from action to outcome simpler. You can simplify the way the innovation works by taking out complication, complexity or effort. You can also simplify the path from action to outcome for the end-user of the innovation. Shallow simplification focuses on ease of use while deep simplification looks at the big picture and at the overall objective of the new idea.

Overcoming is about getting beyond contradictions and conflicts. Your product may offer compromises between speed and fuel consumption, or cost and performance, or size and quality. The innovation that can transcend two conflicting objectives has the potential to increase usefulness without also increasing undesirable costs or side-effects.

Success

People start to build usefulness into their new ideas and look at other people's new ideas to see how they can solve valuable problems. You sit on the boundary between the needs of end-users and the needs of your group.

Localising	Simplifying	Overcoming
▦ How can you adapt innovations to local needs?	▦ Can you simplify the way existing innovation works?	▦ What are the conflicts between end-user goals?
▦ How can perceptions of usefulness be increased?	▦ How can your innovation simplify users' lives or work?	▦ How could you transcend existing contradictions?
▦ Where isn't innovation used because it isn't local?	▦ Do you offer what people don't value? Can you stop?	▦ Can you creatively move beyond constraints?
▦ How can intimate user knowledge create insights?	▦ Do you make people's lives harder rather than easier?	▦ How would things work in a situation without limits?

As your group members focus on creatively improving the lives of others, they will become more open to insights that connect new ideas with old problems. Your people look at the power of new technology – or new methods – and transform them into solutions that are valued by others. You can cut out what gets in the way and what doesn't make a contribution. You can grow with the energy released.

Innovator's measure of success

➤ You recognise the difference between usefulness and newness.

➤ Your team focuses innovation efforts on increased actual and perceived usefulness.

➤ You find new opportunities to localise, simplify and overcome contradictions.

➤ Your efforts actively move from past to present and future innovation curves.

Pitfalls

Some new ideas don't *seem* useful when you first look at them. It can be too easy to reject an idea because you can't see the usefulness rather than looking more creatively at how to make the idea useful. Or you can stay with the comfort of an older idea because it is more useful now. Some people give up on newness because the path to usefulness appears too difficult. The secret is to focus effort on actual and potential usefulness in a series of innovations from now to a more desirable future.

Innovator's checklist

■ Draw up a usefulness/newness grid – or portfolio. Display it in your workplace. Consider the relative benefits and costs of finding new ideas against the usefulness of those new ideas in the short, medium and long term.

- Look at the limits of existing innovation curves. Identify threats from competitors who deliver simpler products. Consider the threats of rising costs within the constraints of existing approaches. How can others disrupt your success?

- Discuss how to increase usefulness of new ideas. Look for opportunities to deliver breakthrough levels of usefulness that will disrupt existing markets (or situations). Imagine new opportunities for creating new markets (or better situations).

- Try to make the difficult, but desirable, possible and profitable. Think about what would happen if you overcome existing contradictions. Consider the impact of delivering something that was five times as fast for half the money. How worthwhile will radical innovation be?

Related ideas

Functional fixedness is about how people can fail to creatively solve a problem because they have fixed assumptions. Research suggests that younger children carry fewer fixed assumptions and can solve certain kinds of creative puzzles more easily. Collections of these assumptions are *mental sets* that tend to limit our creativity over time unless they are challenged and expanded. The way you view objects, people and connections must be restructured in new ways if valuable problems are to be solved. If innovation is about usefulness rather than novelty, new solutions will be found.

One more thing

Nintendo means 'leave luck to heaven'. It believes in focusing on new things rather than competing by doing the same old things. In the president's words, 'if you do the same thing as others, it will wear you out'. Its people find it natural to do what is different. The CEO encourages people to follow what excites them rather than what everyone else is doing.

This dedication to the long-term insight runs deep. Asking unique questions has delivered winning innovations:

Q. Why not put a console in your pocket? A. Gameboy.

Q. Wouldn't cute monsters be cool? A. Pokémon.

Q. Why shouldn't older people use consoles? A. Brain Training software.

Q. How can we get the whole family to play together? A. Wii.

Q. Why not create the world's weirdest console? A. The Wii U.

Q. Why can't we change the world with our ideas? A. Never give up.

Do this now!

Spend 10 minutes thinking about what motivates you to take risks and make new ideas useful

A couple of years ago, Candy Chang, artist, painted a wall with the unfinished phrase: Before I die I want to _____: leaving people to fill in what they would most like to do. There are more than 400 similar walls around the world. I saw my first *Before I Die* wall in Melbourne filled with the hopes and dreams of strangers. Create your own wall at home or work. Watch it fill up.

Grinding your way from insight to (successful) innovation

Insight is necessary but not sufficient. You have to grab hold of interesting insights and help them to become ideas with shape and structure. You need to invent the detail of a practical version of your idea. This can be a flawed prototype but it is part of the journey. The next steps are about whatever is required to make the innovation useful and used in the real world.

Frequency – At the start, and then along the journey.
Key participants – First you. Then, everyone.
Innovation rating: ****

The guys over at Rovio figured out that mobile cartoon style games could be the next big thing. They won a competition sponsored by HP and Nokia while still students in Helsinki. They saw potential in smartphone gaming and decided to gamble on their insight.

Get it right and they would have a blockbuster – their own Mickey Mouse – something huge. They challenged their whole team and worked through thousands of ideas. They wrote 51 mobile games before someone proposed a game with a flock of grumpy birds and lots of coloured bricks.

Angry Birds kept transforming until it became the classic that we recognise now. They focused on getting it to number one in Finland and other small nations before pitching it to Apple via a major publisher. They released a YouTube trailer, many more new levels and a free version. The gaming and marketing innovations kept coming. There were over two billion downloads in just three years.

Objective

As an innovator, it helps to understand the life cycle of innovation. You can predict a lot based on the experiences of many previous innovators. There is a familiar shape with similar activities, roles, tasks, challenges and solutions. At times exhausting, and at times exhilarating.

Pre-innovation often starts a long – or longish – time before you commit serious focused effort to turn ideas into reality. Later, when you look back, the origins of the new idea may seem obvious. Your interests may reveal new opportunities while your frustrations may inspire new insights. New innovations, technologies and systems combine to make possible the previously impossible. External shocks or internal 'aha' moments provoke serious attempts to make innovation work.

Innovation starts with the initial commitment to make the new idea work. There follows an iterative process of divergence – where more options for development are proposed – and convergence – where choices are made between the many possible options. There are many mistakes and failures alongside your successes. Investors and competitors change the criteria for success. People who are involved in the innovation efforts come and go. Prototypes eventually lead to real-world innovations.

Post-innovation is what happens after new innovation emerges. It's the birth of the new innovation and its life cycle including rebirth or eventual death. Production, implementation and operations are necessary to sustain innovation. These operations vary in size (big, small), reach (local, global) and structure (formal, informal). Potential users adopt or ignore innovation while decision-makers and investors, decide how long to support the continued development of the innovation.

Context

It's best to think of the innovation life cycle as a dynamic learning process rather than a static project plan. This makes sense because innovation needs to be about high adaptability that helps you succeed rather than being about doing something difficult just because it's new. Most of the best opportunities will emerge after the serious work begins rather than as part of the original design.

People – including you – create ideas based on experiences, personalities, knowledge influenced by the various cultures in which you live and work. People stimulate new ideas in each other through their words, actions and culture. Some of these new ideas become part of the way society and culture works by adding to – or replacing – the way people behave and think. You – like everyone else – are part of the system for creating the rules and traditions that shape your own actions.

The motivating part of this, for an innovator, is that everything can be changed and improved. You don't have to accept the limits of any way of thinking or behaving. We make the system in which we live, so we can remake our systems and live there: kinder, smarter and happier. This context also explains part of the reason innovation is difficult – because it has to find a place in a human system that already exists. The value of the ideas – their usefulness and their popularity – depends on others.

Challenge

Not all innovation is equal. Innovation can be radical or incremental. Innovation can be applied to different problems. You can innovate services, products, how you do things or what you do. Attempts to innovate can change nothing, small things or everything. You can't know exactly what will happen when you try out a new idea. It helps to think about what you want from innovation.

Each stage of the innovation process involves some uncertainty. The smart innovator asks questions, learns lessons and takes actions to reduce uncertainty. What do the various people involved want from innovation? What kind of innovation do they want or need? What problems are you trying to solve? What solutions are possible or desirable?

Success

You're getting better as an innovator when you understand the main shape and rhythm of the grind from insight to innovation. You can recognise problems and tensions of each stage of the life cycle and anticipate what is likely to happen next. This knowledge helps you prepare other people for highs and lows of progress in a way that protects against complacency or despondency. You expect setbacks and changes in success criteria. You are ready to sell – and keep selling – the new idea.

People become working experts in the innovation life cycle. This allows them to fluidly move into different roles and focus on different parts of the innovation puzzle. They are able to speak the language of creativity and self-manage during the innovation journey. The advantage is considerable if people can see what is likely to happen – or should happen next.

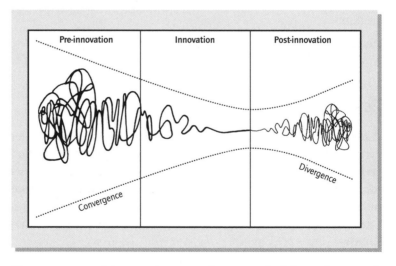

The concepts of innovation turn into practical know-how and then become second nature. Ideas come from everywhere and are developed by everyone. Before insights are shared they are instinctively refined, turned around and examined. When ideas are shared they are nurtured, rather than judged, by conspirators who know how to ask questions and identify the next steps to take.

Fast learning is institutionalised. No-one waits until the end of a project, or a quarter or the innovation life cycle before adapting. Failure, success, the good, the bad and the embarrassing are all used as part of a living experiment into what works, what doesn't and what to try next. Instead of your people being last to know about new trends and waves, they are the first to know – and react.

Innovator's measure of success

➤ You understand the pre-innovation, innovation and post-innovation life cycle.

➤ People know the importance of managing paradoxes at each stage of the life cycle.

➤ Different roles are emphasised at different times to move innovation forward.

➤ Insights are nurtured, developed and challenged by individuals and collectives.

➤ You're working with at least one creative co-conspirator to support your efforts.

Pitfalls

It's tempting to believe far too early that the innovation life cycle is over. You can think that the working prototype is the end of innovation, or the first product to market, or the first innovation to become the dominant design – or new normal way of doing things. People can become complacent about success. Organisations that become famous for being innovative can start to believe their own hype or – even worse – begin to hide behind glories of innovation past. It's easy for the innovative spirit to be overcome by the desire to increase profits and efficiencies – even if the bureaucratic methods of efficiency offer little protection against competition from idea-hungry competitors.

Innovator's checklist

■ People *recognise* the dynamics of the pre-innovation stage. They acknowledge the limits of previous adaptation to previous waves. They know that whatever works now will be unlikely to work in the future. The group actively explore new ideas and divergent new futures.

■ People *understand* the flow of the innovation stage. They share, test and nurture ideas from colleagues at all levels of the organisation – or team. They look outside for help. They openly accept ideas and components from anywhere and anyone that can move insights forward.

■ People do what is *necessary* to exploit the benefits of the new idea. Implementation skills are used along with practical and analytical intelligence. Creativity is not forgotten but applied to different parts of the innovation to make it work and make it popular.

Related ideas

Fuzzy-front-end (FFE) is a term commonly used to describe all the activity that happens before a decision is made to formally attempt a particular innovation. The fuzziness never really leaves as long as you are still attempting to do something new. With innovation there's a fuzzy-middle-bit and a fuzzy-back-end – because you never really know what will work best when trying to do what you and your group have never done before. Some things will become clearer but never everything.

One more thing

The ethical innovator tries to use new ideas for good. This is challenging because the consequences of innovation cannot be fully controlled. Malaria – as an example – kills about one million people each year and has no effective vaccine. People invented mosquito nets and insect repellents to prevent mosquito bites.

To reduce mosquito breeding, some have created insecticides while others encourage the filtering of standing water. In the UK, Oxitec scientists have re-engineered male mosquitoes in an effort to significantly reduce infected insect populations. They have been criticised by several anti-GM groups. Yet, part of the grind is fighting the good fight for ideas that help.

Do this now!

Spend 10 minutes thinking about how to make what you do more useful to other people

You can start with a new idea and try to make it useful. Or you can start with an important challenge, problem or goal, then find new ideas (and old ideas) that will help. Write down stuff you care about, like the team at IKEA who invented a flat-pack house and kept pushing until they convinced disaster relief agencies to use it. What do you want to change? How can you use what you already know?

Measuring (unmeasurable) innovation

The measurement of innovation is paradoxical. It has been argued that to manage something you must measure it first. Yet – it is also true that if you love innovation it must be set free. The effort needed to find useful metrics can bring useful rigour to thinking and provide evidence for change. Too much measuring can actually slow down new ideas rather than speed up revolution.

Frequency – Whenever reviewing or doing design measurement.
Key participants – Leaders. HR. Finance. Marketing. Operations. Those who want to lead.
Innovation rating: ****

3M were famous for giving innovators money and then just leaving them alone to create cool new stuff. Just two output measures were really advertised – the percentage of revenues from new products and their number of patents. The 3M culture was about the inputs to create fabulous new ideas including their famous 15% slack time (available to work on projects that scientists choose) and spending 5% of their revenue on R&D.

When CEO James McNerney arrived, he brought along enough GE inspired efficiency metrics to clog up creative veins and arteries. Too much measurement increased short-term profits but reduced long-term growth. The next two CEOs – both 3M old-timers – reversed the changes. With creative independence restored, numbers of new products soared (25% in 2008, 34% in 2014 with a goal to reach 40% in the next few years). All measurement and no joy makes creativity a chore.

Objective

Measure what helps you innovate more effectively. If you remember the objective, you can choose measures that cost less than they contribute. The cost isn't just about finance. You don't want to lose any speed nor do you want to discourage new ideas.

Calculating is about knowing more about the ingredients, or inputs, that you're putting into the innovation mix. There's the direct investment into creating new ideas and making them useful. And then there's the resources invested into old ideas and protecting them from change. You can count what is spent on training, the creative environment, outside experts and learning about the world.

Monitoring involves keeping an eye on what is being done – more or less in real time. You want to get a sense of how well innovation processes are performing. You can evaluate something about how people feel and whether there is a healthy creative flow from insight to innovation. You can choose to check on different parts of the process – some constant, others changeable.

Reviewing looks at the impact of innovation efforts. There is a purpose behind the focus on new ideas – they are meant to solve problems, improve situations and shape better futures. You can choose between counting new patents, products or suggestions – but the important part is to link, as far as possible, desirable end results with innovation work. Is your innovation strategy working?

If you listened to some people you might think measuring innovation was still fairly straightforward. They would encourage the extensive work of collecting and analysing data without reminding you there is no one best way of counting what matters to innovation.

Context

Try not to measure more than people can manage. Use existing measures and measurement systems wherever possible to avoid wasting time or energy. If you have an employee survey, consider which questions already relate to the effective flow of ideas. If you have a customer questionnaire, think about how successful innovation would change the results. Look for how existing external audits or assessments can be related back to innovation efforts.

You can always add questions or metrics – although it may be better to replace less relevant items than to clog up attention with numbers that are not read or do not improve anything. Even if you are not the person who can make those decisions – you can try to influence. If you are not in a position to influence then you can repurpose existing measures to shape your own innovation contributions.

Measurement is dynamic. Approaches can be listed but that's not the same as telling you which specific measures work for you. The best approach depends on your specific situation and goals. You can use post-project reviews (learning what happened), bench-marking (comparing performance), maturity models (assessing level reached) and balanced scorecards (gaining an overall view).

There is no one dominant stage model. As an innovator, you can make intelligent use of maturity models to get a feel for where your organisation is and where it could go next on its innovation journey. You can also use them to encourage discussion with your people about how urgent and desirable your next steps are. There's something very seductive about seeing that you're at stage number three (for example) and deciding to make changes until you're at stage number four.

The most powerful approach to measurement blends pragmatism with ambition.

It's smart to reuse existing balanced scorecards with an innovation perspective:

- Financials. How can innovation improve the way we appear to investors?
- Customers. How can innovation improve the way customers perceive us?

- Processes. How well do processes contribute to our innovation goals?
- Learning and growth. How can we change and improve through innovation?

The difference is about injecting powerful innovation into the typical mix. More creativity, more ambition, more fluidity.

Challenge

You can link your measures to individual innovations, the innovation process, or to your overall innovation strategy. It's useful to have some specific measurements when making decisions about what to do next, where to invest or how to proceed. There are measurement systems you can buy with more metrics than could possibly be useful. As an innovator, you decide what is important.

You are trying to count many different kinds of uncountable. You will need measurements that help you understand what is happening and how well you are doing. You want metrics to communicate progress. You may also need evidence to convince others to place bets on your gut-feel about the intangible benefits of making unfinished dreams into something real at some point in the future.

Measurement can help people recognise the value of different parts of the innovation process. In part this is because some managers believe that only what is measured matters. You can use this bias towards numbers to highlight the importance of people. The quantitative habit can be used to encourage the qualitative instinct. If you want to encourage exploration then ask questions about how much the future is worth. If you want to encourage innovation then make employee surveys the start of radical change, driven by the creativity of people doing the work, rather than a superficial checkbox exercise.

Success

You'll know you're getting better when what you measure is part of a dynamic model from insight to (effective) innovation. You recognise that measurement is valuable only to the extent that it helps you innovate better. The process of measuring should help you recognise opportunities for innovation, increase understanding of what to improve and let you shape your innovation efforts.

Work-to-measure innovation reveals useful insights.

Innovator's measure of success

- You understand the difference between measurement and improvement.
- Learning is increased each time you cycle through the measurement loop.
- The measurement system is custom-made for your purpose and situation.
- Everyone – at all levels of any hierarchy – is part of the learning process.
- Measurements adapt as needed to help your innovation succeed.
- Unwelcome findings are used productively (and not just ignored).

Pitfalls

Some organisations measure for measurement's sake. They hand the job to an individual or a group who count so many things that people are unable to use the data usefully. Some organisations keep the measurements to a select group rather than sharing it with everyone. It's easy to avoid (open) productive discussion about real barriers to innovation. Defensive routines can move the focus to measuring what doesn't threaten anyone and stop people reaching insightful conclusions. Instead of solving valuable problems, money is wrongly diverted to ineffective measurement systems.

Innovator's checklist

- Consider the various descriptions of the innovation journey (see pages 176 and 185). How far have you travelled? What is working? What isn't working? How fast are you improving? What is about to cause you problems? How effective is your flow from insight to successful innovation? Does your innovation do what you wanted it to do?

- Think about the value gained from innovation. How will you judge success, learning or failure? What is the mix of price, cost and value for any particular innovative product or service? Does the business model match (or help) the innovation to win? Where are there mismatches between improvements in one area and weaknesses in another?

- Look at how you set goals and judge progress. Some great innovators use simple to-do lists and a mental model of how the end-innovation will look and feel. Are there existing corporate systems for measurement? Do they help or hinder? If you get better at innovation, how would the measurements change? How will you judge success?

- Keep your view of innovation effectiveness (or maturity) as clear as possible. What kind of innovation culture do you have? Idea-toxic (kills all new ideas), idea-wasteful (fails to nurture ideas), idea-friendly (welcomes spontaneous new ideas), or idea-hungry (seeks out new ideas)? How effective is your innovation impact? None (superficial or damaging), incremental (minor improvements), radical (major breakthroughs) or revolutionary (huge changes)? Draw a straightforward table assessing innovation at various levels.

Related ideas

The concept of a minimum winning game (MWG) is useful to dynamic measures of innovation (see page 154). The beauty of the approach is that it combines three different ways of measuring innovation into one clear way of knowing what has to be done – and by when. The technique encourages you to consider what goals will follow in the months and years that follow. The same logic can be used for individual projects, products, teams or for the overall organisation.

One more thing

Barbie was first sold by Mattel in 1959. The insight that an adult-shaped doll would be popular came from Ruth Handler who was married to one of the company founders. The insight was ignored until Ruth purchased a similar doll in Germany to convince Mattel to launch something similar. One billion have been sold – with thousands of new ideas needed each year to keep the original idea popular.

Intensive efforts are made to increase the flow of new ideas inside and outside the company. People join temporary innovation teams for three months to mix different skills and perspectives. Social media style networks encourage everyone to share ideas, experience, lessons learned and problems. Employees are connected with external inventors at innovation summits. The measurement is about intensity, effectiveness and richness of collaboration – people working and playing together.

Do this now!

Devote 10 minutes to listing what might stop beautiful new ideas succeeding in the real world ☐

It might sound negative, but it's really one of the most optimistic things you can do. Listing what might stop you – the wall – is how you get serious about getting over the wall to making those new ideas work. What fears do you have about future success or failure? Politics? Resources? Knowledge? Skills? Apathy? Rules? Pressure? Just list them. Confront the wall.

four

Winning with innovation

'Creativity requires the courage to let go of certainties...'
Erich Fromm

As an innovator, you want better ideas to win. There are several different ways of winning with new ideas. You can win by making the new idea work in conceptual or practical terms.

You can win by making the idea useful and popular in the real world. And you can win by using the success of new ideas to renew, transform and re-energise your situation or organisation.

Insight emerges in the inner world. What happens next will follow a predictable pattern. Success depends on how well the actions of the organisation are adapted to their environment.

As problems and possibilities are better understood, you can try to create popular innovations that fit into the life/work of people in the outside world. You can try to make a difference with new ideas.

Your new ideas will compete with existing ideas. Since no idea is ever perfect – or a perfect fit – other new ideas will do battle with your innovations. Novelty will attract attention. Habit will avoid change. Dissatisfaction struggles with satisfaction.

To be a successful (serial) innovator, you will have to increase the perceived usefulness and attractiveness of your new ideas. Ideas need friends.

You can innovate with what you do (product and service). You can also innovate with how you do it (process and culture).

Combining *what and how* innovation with strategic thinking and action allows you to establish a desirable place in the external scheme of things. You can successfully renew, transform and disrupt to create a better world.

Winning and losing with innovation

Innovating is not the same as winning. The pioneer may be first, but not receive the greatest reward. It is commonplace for the newest to be ignored or imperfect. If ignored, someone else can learn how to better sell the new idea to make it popular. If imperfect, someone else can learn how to improve the way it works to exceed your giant leap with one little step.

**Frequency – Consider different games along with strategy.
Key participants – You and your team. Strategists. Leaders.
Innovation rating – Innovation6**

Blockbuster rejected the chance to buy Netflix for $50 million. It doesn't seem such a smart idea now but Blockbuster had won its dominant position renting VHS tapes in retail outlets and didn't see the value in postal DVD services. At about the same time, innovation had made online sharing and downloading of movies accessible to anyone with a computer and a broadband connection.

Netflix recognised video streaming as the next wave of movie distribution but were not the first to launch video streaming services. In the grey market, via peer-to-peer services, people were enjoying sharing movies while YouTube popularised online video watching. As soon as commercial movie streaming became practical, Netflix was ready with an online subscription service.

The company successfully de-emphasised DVD rental services before it seemed necessary. It was willing to sacrifice easy revenue to win a bigger game. It kept returning to the grey market to see what people were downloading before doing their content deals. It understood the changing viewing habits that would lead people to watch box-sets all in one go. It prioritised reliable viewing ahead of slick layouts to beat the competition. So far it is winning. But it's only the start of the game.

Objective

Some people believe they can pick the winning innovation among a bunch of losing ideas. Others feel that they can win regardless of the starting idea. You may focus on filtering the kind of ideas you want. You may decide to develop the kind of ideas you've got into the kind of ideas that work.

Making an idea work is one kind of winning. But it's still not the same as the innovation being used to improve a situation. Being useful is also a form of winning but it doesn't guarantee popularity just as popularity may not bring success or riches. Winning with innovation depends on what you view as success and the actions of many different events that may be influenced but rarely controlled.

There is often a distinction made between innovators and followers (see page 203). The follower is viewed as being at a disadvantage compared to the innovator. But if a follower makes a new-to-the-world innovation work in the world, then are they not also an innovator? This is practical creativity.

In our creative world, there are many first-to-the-world innovations but they are not all equal. Some are radical while some only look superficially new (see page 150). Each idea has the potential to be less or more than the sum of its parts depending on the circumstances where it is used.

Many smart ideas are neutralised by dumb processes. Other smart ideas are ignored because they are wrapped up in unattractive packages. While some smart innovators are just not well placed to protect or profit from their new idea even when attractively packaged and cleverly implemented. As an innovator, you can help by crafting innovations and strategy that win together.

Context

Innovation is about competing ideas. Some ideas win. Some ideas lose. Some become the dominant idea, winning all and used by everyone. If you're well placed, you profit from the popularity of the dominant idea. Over time copycats and improvements take bites out of the profit. And eventually some new idea makes the old idea irrelevant. Profitable novelty becomes unprofitable and unloved.

Winning can be about the when of innovation. You want a stream of innovations that are understood by customers (or users of the idea) *before* your competition. Being ahead of the main players allows you to shape the market for the idea. You create uncontested space between you and competitors. You create safe space for customers who trust you to deliver better first.

Yet the timing cannot be so early that it will not work, steal excessively from past products or fail to interest customers. Or too late to capture attention, impress partners or miss the profits in the idea. Ideas can be too new to be appreciated or too late to get anyone excited. Winning involves timing but it also needs to fit into the situation in which it will be used.

Your idea is on a quest. It must travel from the minds of innovators to the real world of the end-user. Along the way it must jump the conceptual gap, evade the competition, be passed around like gossip and be worth the trouble it causes. You can win through building a better network, increasing usefulness, having complementary capabilities, or by just grabbing hold and growing opportunities.

Challenge

The challenge is to use innovation to move somewhere better. The new idea is used to shape the future in ways that users and creators both find desirable. This is about strategy, figuring out how to use the new idea as your unique means to get to desirable ends. Ideas are seldom useful in isolation and, in a similar way, chains of innovation need to be connected with opportunities and capabilities.

Bloody is what happens when everyone can do what you can do and everyone understands what, why and how you're doing it. The product or service can be very useful but there are few reasons for someone to work with you rather than the next provider. People in this situation tend to try and compete on price, customer service and location. They may also use marketing or legal protection to survive.

Beautiful is a competitive situation where no-one can do what you can do but everyone understands why you are doing it. You're ahead of the pack but they're going to be chasing you down. The benefits of your position and the logic seem obvious enough to be copied eventually. People in this place have to use the clarity of their position to attract partners while looking to maintain their edge.

Paradise is that wonderful place where no-one can do what you can do and (at least) your key competitors don't understand why, what and how you're doing it. Maybe you're offering less than they think customers need or more than they think customers want. The great thing is that people are slow to compete because they don't really get what customers are buying.

Success

You'll know you're getting better at winning with innovation when you see strategic opportunities from your new ideas. Strategy and innovation work best together. You can see strategic gaps that innovation can help to bridge – and then set out to create the breakthroughs you need. You can also see the potential for strategic advantage from innovations that have been created by others.

Innovating is creative but winning with innovation also needs rigorous, disciplined, big picture imagination. If you can develop the ability to think in several dimensions you can prioritise effort in those areas of innovation that will allow you to build up a winning momentum. You will not only think of what *can* be done but what will place you in an increasingly strong position.

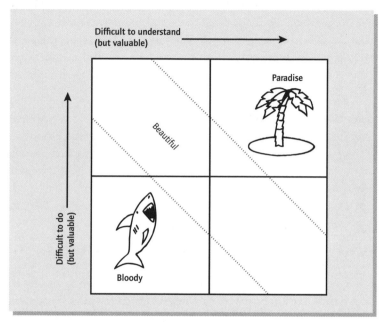

You'll move away from the bloody waters of easy to do and obvious. You'll move towards the paradise of difficult to do *and* difficult for competitors to understand. This is a paradise because what you do is valuable – and often appreciated by those you help – but not easy to copy, or stop. Some of this innovation will be about *what* you do, and some will be about *how* you do it. Moving towards paradise is about doing things so well – or so differently – that no-one else would try it.

You start by redefining what is possible. This eventually changes what is desirable and then acceptable. You now stand alone in paradise. Your competitors can't do what you can do and, at a deep level, they don't understand how, or why, you're doing it. Your customers – or colleagues, or citizens – know they love what you doing and can't get it anywhere else.

> ## Innovator's measure of success
>
> → At least one winning innovation game has been designed.
>
> → You understand what traditional players, innovators and followers are doing.
>
> → Innovations are pursued in an order that makes sense, given the strategy for winning.
>
> → Everyone in the business recognises the interplay between making the idea popular, the innovation work, and the business successful (see page 165).
>
> → People are ready to redirect innovation efforts when better opportunities are found, when competitors establish a winning game or when circumstances change.

Pitfalls

It's a mistake to believe that any innovation is the secret of perpetual victory. Many people have become complacent with the popularity of a successful innovation. The tyranny of success either makes people think that they cannot lose or that they must always win in everything they do. New ideas are expected to immediately deliver the same level of winnings as the original winning idea. Smaller ideas are starved of attention and affection. Any idea that challenges something that has won in the past is discarded because it risks turning a winner into a loser. Competitors are left to fashion new victories from ideas that were considered but rejected by the market leader.

Innovator's checklist

■ Create a roadmap for your innovation with 3–5 stages, or milestones, over 3–5 years.

■ Start your roadmap with the general trends for innovation in your market or external situation. Understand the potential turning points. What would make your innovation easier? What would make your innovation irrelevant?

■ Continue your roadmap by listing the things that need to happen for your innovation to be successful in the real world. How much money do you need? What skills must be found? Which partners do you need? How will you get the innovation to market?

■ Draw the roadmap and stick it up on the wall. Use the various tools and questions in this book to increase your understanding of the path to successful real-world innovation.

Related ideas

The co-founder of Intel predicted that it would be possible for the power of computing hardware to double about every two years. Moore's law helped to organise winning innovation strategies at the company. Moore describes various stages of innovation development and identified an innovation chasm between visionaries and pragmatists. He argues that disruptive innovations benefit from building momentum into a bandwagon effect until your new idea becomes the new standard.

One more thing

Less than a year after Netflix launched its first movie streaming service, Roku launched its own Apple TV style streaming device. Roku switched attention from audio streaming systems and jumped onto the video streaming wave. While Apple sold tight integration with other Apple products, Roku pursued an open content strategy as a way of winning. The innovation strategy is designed to attract partners and customers who want something that works beyond the closed Apple eco-system.

Do this now!

Spend 10 minutes jotting down how the success of your creativity efforts will be measured

You might be measured by financial results. Pay attention to whether traditional return-on-investment metrics (earnings-per-share, fixed versus sunk costs and discounted cash flow) are unfairly devaluing the future value of new ideas. You might measure success based on how well you solve a real-world problem. Or how much fun you have. Or how famous you become. Your choice.

Making innovation popular

Ideas are fashion and tradition. Ideas are solutions. Ideas are trouble. And because they are all of these things, the popularity of an innovation depends on the capriciousness and habits of human nature. The more you understand what makes an idea attractive, the better chance you have of making people make room for your innovation in their lives. Get your idea into hearts and homes.

Frequency – Examine carefully. At least annually.
Key participants – Your team. Your organisation.
Innovation rating:****

Microsoft launched its smartwatch way too early. Its attempt – the SPOT watch – didn't live in a world with a smartphone in every pocket and handbag. Microsoft was also way too late. It built a FM radio network to broadcast weather and traffic updates to its watch but the technology was overtaken by Wi-Fi and 3G. The company did so much right but appealed mainly to gadget junkies. Its approach with versions by Fossil and Swatch was too closed and too slow to find a winning recipe.

Eric Migicovsky launched his smartwatch idea to the wrong people. He tried to convince investors but couldn't get the backing from experienced venture capitalists. Then Migicovsky pitched his smartwatch idea to the right people. He posted his Pebble concept onto the website Kickstarter and asked for cash pledges in return for a discount on the watch when it was built. The watch received a world-record $10 million and 68,000 orders from people who knew exactly why it was a great idea.

The Pebble adds something to innovations that people have already grown to love. It connects to Android and Apple apps via Bluetooth. The Pebble doesn't need to own its own network. And it has thrown the doors open for ideas from anywhere –

particularly fans and friends of the idea that inspired the first generation product. The Pebble offers free software updates to reward customers. It makes it easy – and free – for anyone to develop the apps that keep making the Pebble more lovable.

Objective

You will always be uncertain about which innovations will be successful but you can be fairly certain about how particular innovations tend to become popular. You can use knowledge about the shape of the adoption of new ideas to encourage people to use your innovation. The innovation life cycle is also very helpful in figuring out how to compete with other new ideas now and in the future.

Innovation lovers (innovators)	Early adopters	Early majority	Late majority	Innovation haters (laggards)
The 2.5% who embrace new ideas. They happily invest time, effort and money to play with and test the latest and newest.	The pragmatic 13.5% lead by adopting ideas before they become very popular and show others how useful they can be.	The 34% who pay close attention to early adopters and move some time after they feel innovation is established as the new normal.	The 34% who drag their feet over costs and effort of new ideas. They are suspicious of change and prefer stability.	The final 16% who will use new ideas only if there is no other choice – or after it has been around so long it is now an old idea.

Some of this is about how open – or closed – people are to new experiences while some of it is about the level of their underlying need for the benefits that the innovation promises. As an innovator, you can anticipate the behaviour of different groups. You can adjust your expectations based on gaining a richer understanding of the needs and nature of your target groups.

People can be closed to new experiences in general but recognise their particular need for solutions offered by innovation. Specific need overcomes general attitude. This is important to understand because you can move directly to people who need your innovation – potentially a bigger market – rather than work slowly from innovation lovers to early adopters before reaching the majority.

Context

The momentum that led to innovation must be continued into adoption, use and popularity. This momentum is shaped by many different forces both inside and outside the organisation: the effort of the innovator, how people decide what innovation to use, the way the innovation is shared with the world, and the shape of the human system in which people will use your innovation.

Effort	Decision	Communication	System	Design
Amount?	Criteria?	Mass media?	Fluid?	Advantages?
Intensity?	Timing?	Social media?	Rigid?	Compatibility?
Duration?	Process?	Interpersonal?	Traditions?	Complexity?
Expertise?	Group?	Formal?	Network?	Trialability?
Resources?	Individual?	Informal?	Flow?	Observability

Innovations have to find a place in the world. Some innovations may be independent but nearly all are partly interdependent or completely dependent on how well they mesh with existing ideas. There will usually have to be changes to the innovation or the systems that surround the innovation.

Changes to accommodate the innovation are made by different people. There are people inside the team that built the innovation. And there are people outside the team that built the innovation. Sometimes the direct users have changes made to suit the way that they work. Other groups may build their own versions of the original innovation or build add-ons and companion innovations.

The original innovation is very unlikely to become – or remain – popular without changes. Some of these changes will emerge organically outside of your direct involvement. Others will be deliberately intended inside your direct influence. Successful adoption depends on how well matched – or adapted – your version of an innovation is to its specific environment.

You try to increase the relative advantages, compatibility, simplicity, trialability and observability of your innovation design. Some of this you do through deliberate design efforts and some – if you are smart – you do by looking at what works even if you don't understand why. You can keep digging until you understand more but first use the function to achieve better adaptation.

Challenge

The challenge is moving from the intricacies of innovation to mastering the mechanisms of the market. This can be difficult. People may have forgotten the insights that led to the decision to implement. The individuals who worked on the original projects may have left the organisation or be focused on other ideas. Understanding the fit between solution and problem may fade in time.

Let's be clear. It may only seem obvious why something succeeded *after* it has been successful. The same is true of failure. Knowledge about the precise interaction between environment and innovation popularity is imprecise. Yet some mistakes will almost certainly damage the chances of a particular innovation being successful – at least in the short term.

Failure to adapt is always the biggest mistake. Your initial insight is necessarily flawed. Your first – and last – ideas are unavoidably imperfect. The innovations that you launch into the real world will need to be changed – not just once, but forever. Assumptions of perfection are dangerous – and bewilderingly incompatible with real-world success.

Many adaptation lessons can only be learned outside the laboratory, workshop or office. You need to keep back resources to make changes to the innovation based on what is learned after the launch. Try to launch ideas early enough to leave time and effort for the next few attempts. Launching small and simple also encourages support and advice (rather than reviews and verdicts) from the world.

Success

You're getting better at making your innovation popular when you understand the differences between the various groups and how they think about new ideas. You know what each group can offer you and how not to get trapped trying to perfect your innovation for the wrong group. You can see and get around potential chasms – or gaps – between the needs of each group.

You know that insights and ideas are not a blueprint for success. You deliberately adapt innovation to what you know of the environment. You try to match your promotion efforts and communication to the decision processes and social systems of your target audience. You dig deeper into how your innovation is likely to be used – your people get close to the people who will determine success.

You reject perfect and learn from every imperfect launch. You reduce all-or-nothing expectations. You have beta-programmes to allow innovation lovers and experts to help you look past blindspots and find damaging aspects of design. Your organisation knows that the first version is rarely – if ever – the most successful version and that sustained innovation success requires never-ending adaptation.

Innovator's measure of success

- → You understand that there are different levels of like and dislike for newness.
- → Your team recognise the attributes of each group in your target audience.
- → There is active effort to jumping the adoption gaps between different groups.
- → Innovations are actively designed and redesigned to become popular.
- → Fast learning cycles turn feedback from the outside world into successful adaptation.

Pitfalls

Unfortunately, sometimes the people making the innovation work undervalue the people who have to make the innovation sell. Making an innovation popular isn't just about selling crappy new stuff that no-one wants or needs. Even the most life-enhancing ideas do little good if no-one knows they exist – or if they don't generate enough resources (often profit) to sustain supply of the innovation. It is tempting, but very wasteful, for innovators to step away from the real-world application of new ideas. You need to plug them into the knowledge and opinions of people who put the ideas to work.

Innovator's checklist

- **Consider the stages of adoption**. What stage has your new idea reached? Is your innovation being used by fellow innovators or convinced early adopters? When do you expect to reach the early or late majority? What level of adoption would be a success? Do different groups have very different needs? Can you go directly to the main target group?

- **Increase the attractiveness of your innovation.** Are the relative advantages of your innovation clear to target users? Does your new idea fit into the way people already think and act? How easy is your innovation to understand and use? How easily can people try your new idea? How quickly and easily can people observe the results of your innovation?

- **Find a name worthy of your innovation.** A great innovation deserves a great name. Innovation needs to be remembered long enough to be researched, tried out and passed on to other people who might benefit. Create fascinating stories for fascinating new ideas. Figure out a story for the origin, the founder and the users to make your idea come alive.

- **Get everyone involved.** Make sure the process of making innovation popular is not banished to marketing, sales and advertising. Departments, functions and people need to talk to each other and learn from what's happening. Prepare options for re-engineering, rebadging or redrafting any part of the innovation as fast as possible – preferably instantly.

Related ideas

Recent work on how innovations become popular have explored the complexity of different kinds of social networks and the role of individuals within those networks. The modelling of various diffusion networks lead to some interesting conclusions. *Bandwagon dynamics* suggest that often everyone will adopt a dominant innovation or hardly anyone will bother. This depends on networks that rely on just a few powerful sources of influence who share the same – or similar – opinion. The divergence that leads to innovation must – often – depend on convergence to become popular.

One more thing

Alfredo Moser has been called the 'poor man's Edison'. Facing a black-out in Brazil, he stuck a bottle half-filled with water into a hole he drilled into his roof. Sunlight refracted light through the water lighting up his dark room. Within a few years, the idea had spread to countries as far away as India and Bangladesh. There are now millions of homes with Moser bottle lamps. The idea has spread because it solves a problem in a way that fits perfectly into the lives of those who benefit from it.

Do this now!

Spend 10 minutes thinking about how to increase focus on the situation you want to improve

Getting focus on to a problem is one of the best ways of finding solutions. Like the street-artists in São Paulo, Gabriel Pinheiro and Victor Garcia. They want a more colourful urban environment, so created an online campaign to match graffiti artists with property owners. Think of the healthcare activist in Holland, Beatrijs Janssen, who carries a vendor tray with female condoms. Get attention.

Selling new ideas

Ideas need friends. They also need resources. They need people to develop them into something useful. And then they will need people to use them. Ideas have to be shown. They have to be attractive to others. As an innovator, you will have to sell your insights, ideas and innovations.

Frequency – At the start. Often.
Key participants – You. Innovation team. Then leadership.
Innovation rating: ****

Airbnb offers an internet market that matches private renters with private guests. Originally called Air bed and breakfast, its founders developed the idea after offering short-term accommodation as a way of affording expensive rent in San Francisco. They had to market the idea to their first guests as an alternative to overbooked hotels. They convinced a programmer to join as a third founder.

They sold their new idea to delegates at high-profile conferences. And then guests helped sell their new idea to more guests – and produced an interesting story for journalists covering the events. They pitched their new idea to bloggers with small audiences because they believed they were more likely to pay attention. They produced commemorative breakfast cereals for both presidential candidates – Obama O's and Cap n' McCain's. Each box was sold for $40 to pay off their debts.

They used the presidential cereal gimmick as a way of selling their idea to a world famous investor – Y-combinator. Being accepted by one investor gave them credibility with others including celebrity investor Ashton Kutcher. This helped them sell the new idea to more than 9 million new guests. The new idea has been sold in 11 new countries. The founders are unstoppable salesmen for their idea.

Objective

This is the part about how to sell your new ideas. And where you think about how other people should be selling your ideas if they want to convince you to support them. All along the innovation life cycle, there are people to convince, cajole and capture. Your innovation may die without them.

You will face varying levels of hostility, misunderstanding, apathy, conflict and interrogation. Different individuals in different groups will require different kinds of information, answers to different sorts of questions and different styles of communication – and sales. There's no need to master every nuance but it's helpful to have a working knowledge of how to influence others.

Strategic logic is the hypothesis (or rationale) that justifies your new ideas. It is about good things that will happen if you make this new idea useful. Ideally, it is also about bad things the innovation will avoid. It should be simple enough to allow the audience to clearly see what will be achieved. A single sentence. And a diagram showing your innovation (change) leading to a desirable outcome. It should include risks, blockers and how your audience can help. It's also an invitation to get involved.

Business cases are often requested. The problem is that they demand too much filler and not enough killer, and are best kept light-weight while the innovation is imaginatively explored and reality tested. People who demand formal business plans will usually ask for details of the innovation as a product or service, market opportunity size, target customers, analysis of the competition, pricing, sales, marketing, various risk assessments, financial forecasts and resource requirements.

Show-and-try is about influencing by doing. You experiment without waiting for permission. The spirit of bold invention guides your actions. Learning is more important than pitching. Proving your new idea works is more motivational than filling out forms and documents. You learn how to make or recruit makers to your cause. It's the way of the skunkworks. The garden shed or the garage entrepreneur. You prototype. You sketch. You build. You demonstrate that innovation works before asking for additional resources and submitting to the burden of bureaucracy. People come to you.

Gut evangelism involves the non-formal, emotion-first, relationship-led approach to building a collective around your new idea. You may not even know exactly what form your new idea should eventually take but you want something new to happen. You know some breakthrough is needed. You find like-minded individuals. You find shared problems. You create community around your idea.

You share how you all feel about the need for something different until – through exploration, repetition and signs of devotion – it becomes obvious that something has to happen. And then, usually, a bunch of new ideas emerge from all over the organisation – little, big, ugly, bodacious, silly, daring, quirky and effective. You have helped sell innovation as a way of life rather than any particular product or service idea. People talk, sleep, breath, experiment. You sell by inspiration.

Context

Successful real-world innovation is rarely a simple matter of following formal stage gates between proposal and implementation. This is known in theory but often ignored in practice. Similarly, real-world influence is not as straightforward as presentations in prearranged meetings. Yet it is important to know formal criteria for gaining approval and funds. Even if you move around them.

Knowing about the nature of your innovation goal is important. How incremental or radical is your innovation? Is your innovation mainly about new technology or new markets? Will your innovation produce new services or new products? Knowing something about the climate for new ideas also matters. Are there particular needs? Sources of pain? The answers alter how to best sell new ideas.

Powerful new ideas start as minority opinions about more commonly shared experience. Innovators work to challenge – and then replace – something about the existing situation. Eventually you have to change what is done or how something is done. Selling new ideas is about encouraging change in the direction that makes adopting those new ideas seem like the most natural and logical choice.

To be influential, the innovator has to be flexible while also being consistent. Consistency shows commitment to the new idea which provokes interest from other people. Flexibility stops you being viewed as the enemy. Flexibility allows the new idea to avoid unnecessary opposition where the changes are unimportant to the overall objective of the innovator. Together they are effective.

Challenge

The best path to selling a particular new idea is never identical, but there is a powerful logic to influence. If you don't have power then you will need to develop power or influence someone who has power. If your group demands proof, then you will need proof. It is worth remembering that you don't need to convince a majority but simply to gain the resources necessary to make progress. Some would-be innovators get stuck behind bottle-necks of their own creation. They wait for everything before doing anything.

Maybe you're not the creator of the new idea that needs selling. You could be a colleague. Or an entrepreneur. An investor. Or executive. You may be making the decision about the new idea. You will have your own opinions, preferences and prejudgements about the subject matter or the proposal. When first created, most new ideas are beautiful to the people who have created them and ugly to everyone else. You must (try to) see beyond your bias to the beautiful possibilities.

In an organisation, the objective on all sides of the selling process should be nurturing useful ideas. Not fooling people into saying yes. Or saying no because it makes life temporarily simpler or because it avoids change to existing power structures or traditions. You want to motivate people who are selling ideas to find more convincing arguments. You want people buying ideas motivated to test the real value of an argument. You want people to look behind superficial presentation and collaborate.

Success

You're getting better when your new ideas gain the support they need. You know various principles of minority influence and can apply them naturally – as part of your daily work. You show commitment and consistency (caring about your own idea), offer social proof (who else is doing it?) and make the idea attractive (solving valuable problems and making people look good).

As a leader of innovation, you make the various ways of selling new ideas clearer. Help your people see the difference between deep arguments (central route) and shallow appearance (peripheral route). Some people are so different to the group that wonderful ideas are ignored. Others are so popular with the group that faults are disguised. Both approaches reduce the likelihood of success.

With success, selling, buying and deciding becomes part of the learning process. You pay attention to how people respond to your ideas. You look for people inside group norms who share your belief in the new way. They can become part of team innovation helping you to move around bias to get the idea accepting. You can better understand how to motivate experts to critique and improve your new idea. Selling an idea moves from being a one-shot-trick to the magic of mass experimentation.

Innovator's measure of success

- You understand the key principles to influencing others.
- You know how new ideas get support in your organisation.
- People know the important questions innovators must answer.
- Decision-makers are a positive part of the innovation life cycle.
- Shallow appearance and deep arguments are combined effectively.

Pitfalls

It's easy to believe that to sell something means looking and acting like an extrovert, snake-oil salesperson. This would be a mistake because it discourages introvert innovators from learning how to influence in ways that better suit their talents and personalities. Some people start to see decision-makers as the enemy. Unhelpful caricatures of risk-averse lawyers, stingy accountants and profit-obsessed executives do little to help your innovation to get valuable support and feedback.

Innovator's checklist

- ▦ You know how to sell your new idea. You can influence people who can help make it useful and popular in the real world. You need people in power to make decisions. You will need people with resources to let you build your innovation. You will need people with skills and knowledge to do what you can't do on your own. New ideas must be sold again and again.

- ▦ Find out more about the climate for new ideas. Are people idea-hungry, friendly, wasteful or toxic? What valuable problems do people want to solve? Do leaders respond more to threats or to opportunities? What is the micro-climate in your team or department? Are radical or incremental ideas more likely to get discussion going? Or to turn into action?

- ▦ Cultivate communities. Build relationships with people to test your new ideas and gain new insights. Create connections with people who are inside resource decisions. Understand needs and motivations so that you can improve your ideas, arguments and appearances.

Related ideas

The conversion theory of minority influence, proposed by Serge Moscovici, argues that people often try to reduce conflict between minority and majority opinions. People with new ideas get a lot of attention. If the minority is confident, people in the majority are likely to consider the arguments for and against the new idea. If the arguments are convincing, people in the majority may start to change their minds in private. Over time, private views may emerge in the actions of a new majority.

One more thing

There are many ways to make a new idea popular. One approach is to do something that is easily recognised as important for those who care about humanity. Ashifi Gogo saw counterfeit medicines as a problem worth solving and Africa's mobile phone network as part of the solution. His crew of innovators mapped out how to fix the broken supply chain while he seized media attention. He delivered a memorable TEDx talk in Boston. He wrote an entrepreneurs' journal for Reuters. Ashifi is a perpetual ideas-selling machine. And that's exactly what beautiful ideas need to make a difference.

Do this now!

Enjoy 30–90 minutes learning about how a new invention or idea became popular

There are many wonderful articles, inspirational books and insightful films about breakthrough ideas and the lives of innovators. Immerse yourself in the creativity and happy accidents of progress. Watch the YouTube video of René Redzepi, Danish Chef, receiving his award for restaurant of the year – pay attention to the passion he shares with his team. Find out how the items around you were created and who was responsible. Jot down similarities and differences to your own situation.

Renewing, transforming and disrupting

Innovation is soap opera and adventure. There is always another episode. There are cliff-hangers. Actors with small parts can end up as stars. The big names can be killed off. It's always the beginning of next part of the innovation story. Try to write yourself into the happily ever after.

Frequency – Now. Quarterly.
Key participants – You with your organisation.
Innovation rating: Innovation6

Square is an attempt by the founder of Twitter to revolutionise how we pay. The new idea is to make the payment process almost invisible. The ideal is for payment to happen when convenient for the customer. Everything necessary to pay for a taxi ride would happen *before* the end of the journey. The same would happen for a meal in a restaurant. Or a stay in a hotel. Or visit to a bar.

Existing technologies are combined to make the overall process less disjointed. It is a deliberate attempt to disrupt existing payment providers. The success of the innovation depends on people changing their behaviours *and* choosing Square as their new favourite way of paying their bills. Square must compete against other ideas, powerful competitors and the habits of billions of people.

Square launched with a device to turn a smartphone into a payment card reader. Next came a device to use a tablet as a more complete point-of-sales system. Then an app for customers followed by digital cash. The new idea has found friends over at Starbucks who want to use it to compete with a superior customer experience. The original disruptive idea rarely leads to instant revolution.

Objective

Innovation can renew organisations, transform situations or disrupt markets. The impact of powerful ideas can be felt beyond the immediate way in which they are used. Some consequences of a new idea are unintended by the people who created them – but it is also possible to deliberately use innovation to achieve benefits outside of the immediate benefit to the user.

Renewing is about breathing new life into old organisations. Organisations grow old for many reasons. People may get bored and disinterested in their work because the work never changes. The systems, rules and procedures are the same – but the energy and commitment of people declines.

Alternatively, there is less success because there is a less interest in what the organisation does and how the organisation does it. There is a growing mismatch between what is supplied and what is demanded. This can be because of changing tastes, needs and competition from new and old ideas. In the old world, BlackBerry was the must-have phone; in the new world, it becomes a must-avoid.

The smart leader can reenergise the organisation by developing an innovation of culture (see pages 51 and 144). CEO Ghosn re-energised Nissan, who had lost money for nine years in a row, by channelling the existing creativity of people who already worked for the company. He did the world tour – asking questions, providing the permission and encouragement necessary to break the rules in a culture that had strong conformist traditions. In just 12 months, the company was profitable again.

Transforming is about improving a situation. The objective is focused on making something better inside or – just as often – outside the organisation. FedEx offers carbon-neutral deliveries at no extra cost by investing in more fuel-efficient planes, electric trucks and reforestation projects. Croatian scientists have found a way of getting bees to detect the 1.5 million landmines in Croatia.

The innovator can design something to transform the way people work or live. Like farmer-managed natural regeneration in

Senegal teaching coppicing techniques to renew vegetation that would have once been cleared – enriching soil, saving on fertiliser and doubling crop yields. Or sheep – naturally immune to drug-resistant super-bugs – being nurtured to develop antibodies to fight them. Or Xerox using electronic badges to send patient information to medical staff based on which room they're in.

Disrupting seeks to change how a particular market works. Traditionally, this is done by providing a simpler solution that – by undercutting the market leader – increases the number of customers (see page 182). High-cost providers shrink while low-cost providers grow. Like IBM exiting the PC market it helped to create and selling its business to Lenovo in China. And it's not necessarily innovation-led.

Innovation-led disruption is different. You may find a new way of making money – often described as business-model innovation. You sell in a different way – like Amazon versus Borders. You could disrupt markets with product innovation. You package up existing ideas in a different way – think of American Airlines versus Southwest Airlines or Virgin. Or you find a new technology – like 3D printing in the home versus mass production in factories. There may be ripples or revolutions.

Context

Before recognising the need (or desire) to renew, transform or disrupt, there is almost always a build-up of stress and pressure to do something. Real-world performance may be going down or real-world competition may be going up. Stagnation may have set in so that individuals are no longer being promoted and salaries are no longer being raised. There is dissatisfied chatter at all levels.

There is a period of deciding-to-decide, pre-innovation or gestation during which many different things may happen. People may be very open to change or grudgingly open to change. This willingness to consider change may fade away. Any appetite to embrace innovation may be temporary so make sure you use the moment intelligently. Don't be wasteful with crisis or desire.

Under pressure there is a temptation to choose between what is already known: projects, plans or proposals that people have probably discussed. People may follow approaches to change that are traditional – rather than creatively exploring powerful alternatives.

As an innovator, you need to refill the *garbage-can* of existing options so that it becomes an *idea-basket* for future success. Leaders can only make decisions based on available options. When there is a problem they reach into the garbage-can of existing alternatives even when those alternatives are not really solutions to the problem they face. Providing new alternatives, new examples from other companies, new technologies and new concepts you can improve creative problem-solving.

Challenge

The challenge is to help the group imagine alternative futures. You want to find opportunities that go beyond the obvious options. If you have the time – and reserves – then get hold of resources to learn your way to innovation-based renewal, transformation or disruption.

Like Disney CEO Eisner who held bring-your-weirdest-idea breakfast meetings and competitions to find the ideas that became the engine of growth for the next 30 years. Or CEO Gerstner who asked for an army of volunteers to build the new IBM. Or Ford CEO Mulally who shared his passion for 'contributing something really important', first at Boeing and then Ford. In each case, the approach of the innovator was to build a bigger brain of engaged people in a climate of adventurous creativity.

There is typically a lull after a decision is finally made about what to do next. Moving into action can also mean moving back into standard roles, departments and rhythm. People return to business as usual as they get on with development or implementation. Some new ideas run out of energy, some lose their focus and others fail to adapt and grow. If there is enough failure, the pressure returns again and the whole cycle begins again.

The danger is that nothing has really improved. Instead people have wasted time and resources without finding sources of new prosperity.

As a leader of innovation, you start a more iterative cycle of learning and growth. This kind of positive adaptation is more likely to be successful when it is not an isolated, one-time product or service improvement. You want people thinking about a stream of innovation. You want people working creatively on how to make the innovation successful, and on what happens next.

Success

You're getting better at using innovation to renew, transform or disrupt when you think of innovation as a means to an end – rather than an end in itself. Creativity can be highly motivating but you also create in order to achieve other goals. Your organisation doesn't isolate the innovative gene but instead encourages it to alter the way that people feel, think, dream and work together.

Success is about deep innovation rather than superficial creativity. The details matter. Design matters. The colours on the walls and the pattern on the uniform can make a difference. But as a smart innovator, you know that these ideas are more powerful when they are brought together, joined up, to become something cumulatively worthwhile. The organisation is forever young.

Innovator's measure of success

- Recognise the potential of innovation to renew, transform and disrupt.
- Use external pressure or internal desire to encourage exploration of the future.
- Identify specific opportunities for innovation to renew the organisation.
- Find situations that you can transform with innovative ideas, products and services.
- Your people see the organisational life cycle as a perpetual cycle of innovation.

Pitfalls

It's tempting to believe innovation will lead to success – or renewal – without solving the reasons the organisation is failing – or declining. Your people may be more open to innovation but not more effective at using innovation. Your leadership may be willing to invest in new ideas but be far too narrow in the scope and scale of those new ideas. There may be a desire for breakthroughs but not enough money or time dedicated to jumping strategic gaps. Crisis can stop people thinking openly and discourage the kind of empowerment that people need to do their best innovation work.

Innovator's checklist

- Encourage confidence in the future. People need to feel they are facing motivational challenges rather than hopeless threats. Reduce excessive pressures because they will reduce creativity. Keep – and attract – the powerful innovators who will seek new opportunities elsewhere if they don't see a good use of their talents working with you.

- Create slack resources for innovation. Desire for better performance can lead to emphasis on efficiency and cost-cutting that stop people from innovating. If people have no time they can't do the playing, testing, talking and thinking that innovation requires. Be smart with money without killing future prosperity. Don't eat the golden goose to reduce the food bill.

- Use innovation strategically. Strategy is about shaping the future. Innovation gives strategy new options for shaping a better future. Strategic innovation is about doing two things at once. Focus creativity on solving existing strategic problems *and* react to the new opportunities that insights, ideas and innovation make possible. Both – at the same time.

■ Apply the powerful lessons throughout this book. Surf innovation waves. Nurture your creative genius. Be prepared to give up old ideas for better ideas. Create an innovation culture with a better, bigger brain. Build a highly adaptive organisation with motivated people focused on winning by making new ideas useful in the real world.

Related ideas

Renewing, transforming and disrupting are all forms of high adaptability. There are three steps involved in the high adaptability RUN loop. First, *recognise* the need to adapt. Second, *understand* the nature of the adaptation required. And third, do what is *necessary*. For the innovator, the objective is not to just deliver a new project or launch one new idea. The goal is sustained success with a sequence of making points – rather than breaking points – gained by rapid, deep learning.

One more thing

The first 30 years of Campbell's was canned fruit, vegetables and meat. This changed when a newly hired MIT-trained chemist transformed the future of the company by injecting the innovation of condensed soup. The famous red and white labels were inspired by Cornell's football team. Capturing 50% of the market came from buying food ideas and wrapping them in marketing ideas. The company seeks to understand each new generation to craft soup innovations that works with changing habits. Microwavable soup clothed in millennial colours. New ideas keep the company young.

Do this now!

Make a commitment to yourself to make innovation matter in your work or community

Samsung makes innovation matter as part of its sustainability efforts. It believes thriving in the future depends on building a creative organisation. Part of this is a publicly available report describing its progress moving from a time-management culture to a creativity-oriented culture. According to Hyun-Sook Kim, developer of the bubble washing machine, its efforts are about increasing 'open-minded thoughts and perspectives'. Start with your personal commitment.

Surfing waves of creativity

Some people believe that creating is an entirely predictable journey. Other people think that innovating is an impossibly random adventure. The smart innovator knows that 'both' is usually the magic answer. The wave from insight to innovation has a certain shape but what that shape will be on any particular day is uncertain. The smart innovator learns to surf *and* shape.

Frequency – Make surfing part of your day-to-day.
Key participants – First you. Then, everyone.
Innovation rating: Innovation6

The students, Evan Spiegel and Robert Murphy, didn't invent the internet. Nor did they invent the smartphone. They didn't create the idea of sharing funny or intimate moments – humans had been doing that from before they had developed language. What they did was surf, and shape, the photo sharing wave by creating Snapchat. They proposed it as part of a Stanford university assignment. And it was ridiculed.

Undeterred, they did all the work in their living room. They focused on making it as easy, and cool, as possible to just share time-limited photos. They knew photos were a (valuable) thing. They made temporary photos a new (valuable) thing. Within one year, there were more than a billion photos shared. Within two years, Snapchat was valued at $3 billion. They surfed the wave.

Objective

It's not possible to control the largest waves of change. They're bigger than any society, nation, firm or individual. There are huge mega-trends that drive human history along. The exact timing and detail of each wave is unknown, although they tend to have similar shapes. As a result, it is smarter to learn to surf, and shape, than to try and stop them.

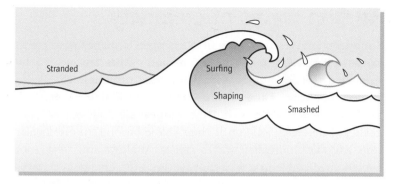

Surfing is all about recognising and then catching the wave. You need to pay attention to the weather, the trend and the patterns. You play with the latest toys, games, movies, gadgets and ideas. You use historical perspective to see the direction and shape of waves. Coca-Cola employs anthropologists to help it understand the potential evolution of societies and behaviour.

Shaping is about trying to change the shape of the wave by changing the shape of the ground (or market) so that it suits your particular surfing style. If you can influence the final dominant design of an innovation that everyone uses, then you are shaping the wave. Google almost gives away the Android operating system because it helps them build search solutions, its main revenue source, into 90% of the world's smartphones and tablets.

Stranded is where you get left behind by the wave. Eventually you'll be so far from where the action is that you will fade away. Often your speed decreases and you become less certain of what direction to make your changes because you're no longer guided by the wave. Borders so misunderstood the internet wave that they handed over its website to key rival Amazon.

Smashed is what happens when you try to stand against the power of the wave. It can also happen when you get left behind and the next wave catches up with you. Or you might be first to come to market and then tread water, too scared for the kind of commitment needed to surf the wave successfully. Think of BlackBerry failing to embrace the power of the touchscreen wave.

Context

Innovation waves can vary in their speed, shape, power and pattern. The most powerful innovation waves are created by connected sets of human behaviours and impulses. The desire to communicate or the need for security. These deep pressures lead to individual waves that may appear random but are – in reality – merely chaotic until their shape becomes more regular and episodic. Individual waves can be shallow and weak – or merely predictable in a way that require little change. Or waves so turbulent that everything in its path has to deliberately adapt or be unavoidably destroyed.

When society, cultures, markets and individuals all stop keeping the rules and following traditions, there is *runaway change*. No-one knows exactly the shape that the future will take but you can be certain that disruptive change will create opportunities for innovators and threats for others. In other circumstances there may be controlled, independent or stable change – all of which offer different threats and opportunities to those who provoke innovation or defend the status quo.

Each wave tends to be cumulative and to replace previous waves. Old ideas are replaced by new ideas. Old technology is surpassed by new technology. Progress follows s-shaped curves with old replaced by new, and new replaced by newer. As an innovator, you can learn to surf, and shape, the s-curves.

There is no future in the past – although there is some past in the future. This means that if you look backwards, you can detect embedded patterns of human need and behaviour. Successful revolutionaries, breakthrough thinkers and social innovators tend to be interested in the history and evolution of humanity. They are not constrained by what has already happened. Instead, smart innovators look for clues that allow them to more powerfully shape and reshape the future.

Challenge

When to bet on the future?

Your gamble will depend on your appetite for risk, your desire to make a difference, and your creative confidence. Timing depends on several things: urgent threats, preparation level and sufficient resources. If you run out of time, you may have to bet desperately. If you have time and resources, you can gamble safely.

What to bet on the future?

There are many different uses for innovation. So it makes sense to develop innovations that fit your situation and facilitate your objectives. Innovation can be radical, incremental, involve technology advances or none, new markets or not, change how money is made, alter networks, improve processes, increase performance or offer better experiences.

How to bet on the future?

There are many ways of organising people for practical creativity. You can depend on a creative (or not so creative) elite whose ideas are followed to the last flourish and icon. You may believe that new ideas come from everywhere and that innovation is more powerful when everyone is involved. There are also many ways of using strategic innovation to shape the future. Strategy can support innovation while innovation supports strategy.

Success

You're getting better when you can recognise the power, shape, speed and direction of change in your situation. You know (some of) the new threats from new technologies and new competitors. You are actively working on opportunities created by change. People openly discuss different responses to social, commercial and technological waves. There is an active flow of trends, fads, fashions, gossip, art, business and theory inside and outside the organisation. You start to shape and surf waves.

Innovator's measure of success

→ You recognise significant waves of innovation.

→ You understand the benefits of surfing, and shaping, waves.

→ You're plugged into the new ideas that will shape the future.

Pitfalls

Some people deliberately reject what they don't understand. They may struggle to see the influence of big waves in the past. They may find it hard to see how waves will offer new opportunities and threats in the future. Even if people see the principles of waves, they may be cut off from the trends, fashions and engines of change. That's why it's so important to use the tools in this book to see how waves of innovation can disrupt or deliver success. An innovator should be a world-class surfer.

Innovator's checklist

- Identify the key waves that are shaping your environment.

- Think about the speed and shape of change in your market or situation. Is change out of control? Is change predictable? Do you have the time to make innovation bets? Have you run out of time to research more new ideas? Do you have the resource necessary?

- Consider the appetite and ability for innovation in your group. Are your people only comfortable with incremental innovation? What would you like to radically improve? What part of your work or your customers' lives needs innovation the most?

- Discuss how capabilities become liabilities. Is your success as part of one wave going to cause failure when faced by a new wave? Use the OODA loop (see page 239) to examine how you can react faster and smarter to new waves.

Related ideas

Nikolai Kondratiev, an economist executed by the USSR for his radical new ideas, argued that capitalist economies have waves of around 50 years of expansion, stagnation and recession. These waves interact with innovation revolutions. New ideas emerge (irruption) and increase prosperity until people get too excited about the new ideas, leading to a bubble followed by a bust. Waves of revolution include the industrial, railways, engineering, mass production and telecommunications.

One more thing

Surfers used to slip off their boards, swim to retrieve them and freeze in cold water. Now they apply wax to give them the grip to ride monster waves, attach neoprene leashes to keep their boards close if they fall, and use special suits to stay warm even while surfing in the Arctic.

The *idea for board wax* came to Alfred Gallant Jr. when he felt the pull on his bare feet from his mothers' newly waxed floor. Popular among those in the lifestyle, it was eventually mass-produced by big brands built around the original insight. The *leash idea* was prototyped by Pat O'Neil, from surgical cord. It was so dangerous that it sprang back and blinded Jack O'Neil, his father, in one eye. But they kept going until the design was a safe part of everyday surfing.

Hugh Brandner, a Berkeley physicist, had the idea for the modern wetsuit. William Bascom, an engineer, proposed using Neoprene. The idea stalled until repeated experiments from Jack O'Neil led to the O'Neil wetsuit company. *Many* brains made the innovations useful. And the combination of innovations made surfing accessible to many more people – enabling more people to surf and greatly expanding the market for further innovation. Combining new ideas revolutionised surfing.

Do this now!

Spend 10 minutes thinking about different kinds of innovation and what you want

Some innovation is a quick fix, some takes a lifetime of dedication. Some new ideas are new products or services while other new ideas bring revolutions in the way people live or think. Do you want small innovations that can be accomplished in minutes, days or weeks? Do you want to be part of huge innovations that will require major funding or significant patience, time and effort?

five

Innovator's turning points

'Innovation distinguishes between a leader and a follower.'
Steve Jobs

Innovation moves from recognising the need – or desire – to adapt, to understanding the kind of adaptation required before finally successful adapting as necessary. You need to encourage dissatisfaction, support experimentation and shape opportunities for transformation.

There are many ways of moving from insight to improvement and because these cannot always be captured in a model or framework, it is important to learn from what innovators actually do – and *how* they focus, feel and think.

You begin with individual creativity, continue with groups of collaborators, and then contribute by making a positive difference to the world. That's why, in this part, it is worth looking carefully at the case notes to get a deeper sense of the energy, purpose and choices of real-world innovation.

At each of these turning points, there are choices to be made and actions to be taken. And those choices, and actions, must be made to shape a future that has not yet happened. And because the future is uncertain, you must depend on principles not rules.

Some people will tell you innovation is all about saying 'no' to what doesn't matter, the way that Steve Jobs claimed he did. Others will tell you that innovation is about saying 'yes', the way Richard Branson claims he does. The truth is that innovation is a blend of yes and no, and a thousand maybes.

The examples are designed to get your mind dirtied up by the messy world of real-world revolutionaries. You can get a sense of the exhilarating decisions and endless possibilities. And how what you say, how you say it, what you do, and how you do it, shapes innovation big and small, failure and success.

A beautiful idea is never perfect

While failure can lead to success, success can also lead to failure. This tends to happen when priorities get mixed up; instead of focusing on making something better, the focus becomes profit, or market share, or defending what you've already got, or the way you've always done it.

At the turn of the 20th century, the factory of Ignaz Schwinn, German immigrant to the USA, benefited from a wave of enthusiasm for the bicycle in its golden age. With the world's first practical pneumatic tyre, a rear freewheel and coaster brakes, the world pedalled and sales soared.

Millions of bicycles were sold and many millions made by manufacturers, with big profits for bike shops, including one owned by the airplane-inventing Wright Brothers. Schwinn became the best-selling, best-known and best-loved bicycle brand in the USA. Today, it still has nearly 90% brand recognition.

Schwinn's success was based on a series of innovations, including a low-cost model that helped it ride out the great depression, the Aerocycle designed to look like a motorbike, and the iconic Stingray inspired by surfing a street-trend for customising bikes with banana seats, ape-hanger handlebars and 20-inch tyres.

Its failure came from a series of anti-innovations, including its obsession with cutting out independent bicycle shops. Distracted by anti-trust litigation, seduced by the easy-money of advertising directly to kids, and strikes from dissatisfied workers, Schwinn management missed three important waves and was left stranded – out of touch with the source and shape of new ideas.

The first wave came from growing interest in touring bikes, lightweight models imported from Europe and then Japan. Not interested said Schwinn. The second wave was the BMX craze from Southern California. Schwinn was late to the wave and then offered an inferior product.

The third missed wave followed the, unbelievably dumb, decision to ignore the insanely popular emergence of mountain biking – a sport developed in Northern California from inventive outdoor cyclists using – wait for it – the frames of old Schwinn bikes with new bolted-on BMX parts. It was an epic fail.

Innovation turning points

→ Identify various turning points in the Schwinn story. How many turning points were there? What would you have done if you were in charge?

→ What turning points has your organisation faced in the past? What turning points is it facing now? What turning points should it be dealing with now – this very moment, or yesterday, or in the very near future?

→ Where did Schwinn's success come from? What smart innovation decisions did Schwinn make? Which waves did it surf successfully?

→ Why do you think it missed three opportunities for innovation? How can you avoid making similar anti-innovation mistakes?

→ What distractions might lead you away from innovation? Are you more worried about stopping competitors or out-innovating competitors?

→ How can you get closer to trends, fads and fashions? Who is innovating? Where are they innovating? Why are they innovating? How can you spend more time with people who are thinking and being different?

→ Would you have been brave enough to argue differently to the rest of the management team? Or disagree with your own leadership?

→ Would you have left Schwinn to start a new mountain-biking or BMX brand? Are you ready to gamble everything on a new idea or huge wave that your market, team or organisation is ignoring?

Related ideas

If you're led only by people who are worried about making money this quarter but are closed to the experiences necessary to creating a successful future, then you *should* be worried about the future. They will tend to over-exploit what they have and under-explore what they could have, with the result that they lose both (see page 227). You need people who see the risk in doing nothing.

Little differences make a big difference

To contribute to a better world, you need an idea worth solving. Some of this is about, to quote Edison, looking for what the world needs and then inventing it. To allow your idea to flourish, you also need it to be used. The other part is about how best to free your idea to improve the world.

Newly married, naive and educated, a villager in a traditional rural Indian area, Arunachalam was appalled to find his wife using cloth rags instead of sanitary towels. He discovered his wife, like other women in India, prioritised food for the family rather than her personal health.

The UN estimates that only 12% of Indian women use sanitary pads, while 70% of reproductive diseases are caused by poor menstrual hygiene. Arunachalam decided to design and make a low-cost sanitary towel to solve the problem. His initial efforts to find volunteers to test his prototype were not welcomed by his family or community. He even wore his own sanitary towel to test its design.

Traditional reticence to discussing menstruation didn't help. The village turned its back on him. His wife left after 18 months of marriage. His mother deserted him. Arunachalam had to uncover trade secrets embedded in the cellulose materials and production of high-tech towels. Eventually, after four years, he successfully developed a four-step method and simple-to-use machine.

The Indian Institute of Technology applied for a patent on his behalf and entered the invention into a national competition which he won. His winner's medal was presented by the Indian president. Since then, his wife returned to help him build a network of home-workers in 100 countries and gave a wildly popular TED talk saying he had 'accumulated no money, but much happiness'.

But Arunachalam was not the first to market. Indian women were not the first to find unsatisfactory solutions. The first commercially available sanitary towels were sold in the 1880s by Johnson & Johnson, developed from technology invented by Benjamin Franklin. There are also simpler alternatives, like reusable menstrual cups, available in apple-like, brightly-coloured silicon.

Innovation turning points

→ Identify various turning points in the Arunachalam story. How many turning points were there? When could he have given up? What next?

→ What is the value of paying attention to problems? What problems do you face in life and at work? What causes you dissatisfaction? Where can you plug into the energy of dissatisfaction of the people around you?

→ How do you feel about Arunachalam's contribution? When can old ideas become new ideas? How can you customise old ideas to solve problems in new ways? Should you patent your idea? Share it? Profit from it?

→ What should you do if you find a better solution than your new idea? Would you give up because someone does it better? Could Arunachalam adapt menstruation cups to his home-factory approach?

→ Has anything in your world – or market – become too complex for purpose? Is anything still too unreliable? Or too expensive? Can you explain an existing innovation better to a new group of people?

Related ideas

Waves of innovation emerge from human creativity and desire. As an innovator, you become a surfer of s-curves. As described well by the problem-solving techniques of TRIZ, your new ideas make a contribution at various points of increasing ideality. Every system, everything, every component can be improved. People make a new idea work, then make it work properly. You maximise performance, then efficiency, then reliability and then minimise cost.

Innovations don't necessarily happen in this order but they tend to follow the curve, until a new curve is needed or discovered.

Many new s-curves emerge as simple ideas become complex, and complex inventions are simplified. Think of smartphones encrusted in diamonds and iguana leather that are sold for thousands, *while* indestructible Mozilla smartphones are sold in Africa for $25 and less.

Sometimes you have to gamble everything

Some innovations need all your commitment. Some breakthroughs demand all you have. Any less than everything, and they have no hope of working. This isn't about winning at all costs, but it is about gambling enough to make your new ideas work. It about placing bets sufficient to change the world.

At the age of 19, Elizabeth Holmes decided to drop out of Stanford University after gaining the insight that advances in micro-fluid technology revolutionise blood testing. She gambled on her insight and ended up living in the basement of some graduate students as she developed her ideas, filed a patent, and looked for the funding to make a revolution in healthcare possible.

Elizabeth had 'enough to know that it *could* work' and was willing to carry out a 'hundred thousand experiments' until she found something that *would* work. She was ready to be turned down by 200 people before finding that investor who believed in her. And with that investment, she found people to run experiments before replacing many of them with people who could execute the plan.

Her new company, Theranos, wanted to radically disrupt the existing market. It takes small amounts of blood with pinpricks rather than needles. Its people invented new devices to automatically test micro-samples in only four hours, for half the cost – publicised clearly – and changed the experience while also saving hundreds of billions of dollars over the next 10 years.

The company plans on offering a home monitoring system to monitor blood in real time so that diseases can also be monitored. Medical professionals and patients will be able to access results via smartphone applications and have their samples picked up for testing at centres no more than five miles away.

Ten years later, Elizabeth Holmes, following in a long line of university drop-out innovators that includes Steve Jobs, Michael

Dell and Bill Gates, was finally able to launch her first services in partnership with Walgreens, the largest drug retailer in the USA. Her board includes Henry Kissinger and she claims to have reinvented healthcare standards by reinventing the blood test. We will see.

Innovation turning points

Identify various turning points in the Theranos story. How many turning points were there? What would you have done differently or the same?

How did Elizabeth get her big new idea? Where did the insight come from? Where do your insights come from? How can you get more?

What are you doing with your most valuable insights? Which insights need to be protected via patents? Do you believe in your new ideas so much that you are willing to commit to them? Are you willing to fail a hundred thousand times to eventually succeed?

Are you interested in long-term, medium-term or short-term innovation? Has your organisation got an innovation portfolio of some kind? Are you doing too little exploring of new ideas? Or too much?

How can you find more time to focus on making your big new idea work? What could you stop doing? How can you divert money from things that don't matter to the things that have to be done?

Who can help you with your new idea? Who can give you advice? Who can give you capital? Who can test your assumptions? Who can build or make what you need? Are you willing to ask until you find answers?

Related ideas

Protecting new ideas through patents can be a hugely important part of innovation success. Deepak Somaya, business professor at the University of Illinois, describes several different patent strategies. The *proprietary* strategy aims to create a portfolio of many patents that cover the entire market opportunity. The *defensive* strategy uses patents to create freedom without being stopped by other patent holders. The *lateral* strategy wants to charge other people for using the new idea rather than stopping them.

Leaders get the innovation they deserve

Innovation tends to happen beyond the unacceptable gap between reality and expectation. If you can divert energy from failing with old ideas to succeeding with new ideas, you can perpetually surf waves of creativity. As an innovator, you can nurture experimentation and provoke imagination.

'I need 5,000 volunteers,' declared Gerstner, new CEO of IBM. He inherited a multi-billion dollar loss and wrote to employees asking for the 'guts to go above, below, around or through internal hurdles'. He wanted innovators 'willing to take risks in the face of conventional wisdom'.

He saw, as an ex-customer and outsider, that new attitudes and new expectations were needed. IBM cleverly distinguished between hot (speed, team-work, new thinking) and not (dress codes, bureaucracy, and slide decks).

Inspired by this call for volunteers, two front-line network administrators decided to help IBM see and grab opportunities provided by an amazing idea – new born and immature – the worldwide-web. Working with an executive, with the influence to get resources, they secretly built IBM's first website.

The IBM website was *not* the idea of the new IBM CEO. But the informality of the leader encouraged informal creativity to deliver what came to be known as e-business. The company grew together *with* the web. Rebel thinkers were attracted to skunk works, under-the-radar innovation projects, and then went back into the organisation to establish them as business-as-usual.

Re-energised IBM jumped head first into new problems with the confidence to transform them into stunning new solutions. Since then, IBM has produced more patents than any other firm. It reinvested in Deep Blue, the chess-playing computer, and Watson, artificial intelligence, that beat the quiz show *Jeopardy*.

IBM people jumped off technology waves – like laptop manufacturing – that didn't match its ambitions. And – critically – IBM understands each new wave is another opportunity for successful adaptation. Its people have fearlessly pursued deep innovation, openly sharing ideas with a world of creative obsessives. It's been an epic win.

Innovation turning points

Identify various turning points in the IBM story. How many turning points were there? What would you have done if you were in charge?

Do your leaders know what will work in the future? Do you know what will be successful in the future? What should you do if you don't know?

Does everyone agree on where to place your innovation bets? Are your gambles on the future too safe? Do you need to spread your risks?

Why do you think IBM grabbed so many opportunities for innovation? How can you see – and grab – innovation opportunities for growth?

What messages do you send about what is needed for future success? Do you make it clear what kind of behaviours are 'hot' and which are 'not'? Do you help give breathing and believing space to would-be innovators?

Where are your innovation volunteers? Can you move beyond the usual suspects for new projects? How are people selected now? Does it work? Can you do better at combining insider influence with outsider insight?

What was the value of IBM's tradition of stealth innovation? Why would you encourage this kind of no-permission prototyping? What about live prototyping in the real world? How do you experiment with the future?

What trends are moving faster than your growth? Can you plug into those forces? Can you sponsor research? Create a maker-lab where people can play with ideas, parts and things? Invest in something fun?

Related ideas

Playing safe can be dangerous. Ronald Klingbiel, strategy professor, uses real options theory to argue that the breadth of innovation gambles is important to avoid too many bets of the same kind based on the same assumptions. We don't *know* what will work, so it makes sense to develop broader innovation expertise that will allow the inevitable losses to be balanced out by big wins.

part

six

The innovator's toolkit

'In a world of change, the learners shall inherit the earth, while the learned shall find themselves perfectly suited for a world that no longer exists.'
Eric Hoffer

Innovation is about practical creativity. It follows that innovating is not the same as innovation tools or models. Yet, these tools can provoke valuable new ideas and help you make those ideas useful.

In this section, as with *The Strategy Book*, I have chosen a personalised selection of tools and models for creativity, problem-solving, change, strategy and innovation. There are some of the more popular tools – used most often in the workplace. There are some of the classic models – those most influential in various fields of creativity, psychology, economics that deal with innovation.

People who have never used the tool before can get almost immediate benefits and insights while continued, creative use of the tools can increase their value. It is also true that many (probably most) successful innovations *do not use* formal tools but they do follow the patterns the models show.

You can make a powerful difference by using better creative and strategic thinking about innovation in your life, job and for your team, department or organisation. Innovation is about bringing new ideas into the real world. Smart innovation is about making new ideas useful.

Draw them first to see how the different parts of the model work together. Add details about your situation or new idea. Use one colour for the model and another colour for your own ideas. Share the models with other people to increase understanding of how new ideas can be made useful.

Creating (smarter) new ideas

Altshuller's innovation pyramid

Not all new ideas are equal. And so it's useful to think about what kind of innovation you want *and* what kind of innovation your new idea might eventually become. You can't be sure that a revolutionary idea will lead to a revolution, or that an idea that doesn't seem new won't one day change history. But you can learn to better understand the ways in which innovation has an impact.

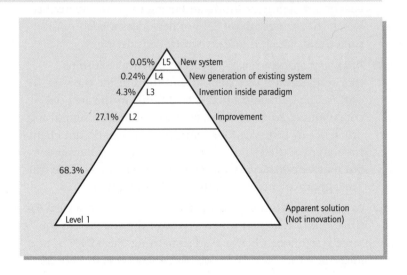

Innovator's insights

An important question about any particular new idea is whether it makes anything better. It may not be as new as you think, or it may not be as useful as you think. That doesn't mean that new ideas should be rejected but that, eventually, they will make varying levels of contribution from (shallow) nothing to (deep) everything. As an innovator you will want to understand the difference.

■ *Apparent Solution* is something that might seem new but isn't actually new and doesn't make any improvement over existing ideas or solutions. You have to be careful here. You could waste a lot of time making your own idea work without giving you any advantage. About 68% of new ideas are like this, so check to see whether you can use what already exists first.

- *Improvement* is something that improves the way an existing approach already solves the problem. The way of thinking about the overall solution has not really changed that much but there's little doubt that it's better in some specific way. The challenge here is figuring out whether the cost of developing, learning and using the improvement is worth the benefit. About 27% of new ideas *would* improve something, which is already worth considering.

- *Inventions* are new ideas made into practical solutions that really make a contribution but from inside the way of thinking (paradigm) that is traditional in the area of contribution. Some 4% of new ideas can make a significant difference (if turned into inventions) but they do not change the nature of the system. This is a significant achievement but may be outside of your focus (or expertise) to make real. They improve only part of the existing situation.

- *New generation* brings new insight into the whole system (or situation) rather than simply a part of the system. It's the same system, only better. And something like 0.24% of new ideas have that capacity to deliver a new generation of an existing system.

- *New systems* are entirely new. They may have similar inputs and similar outputs but they solve what they solve in a new way. Compared to the old system, they are different. Because they are different, they may be rejected by people who don't understand them or would lose because of them. Because they are so new, they may come at the cost of significant learning, preparation and improvement before they perform better in the real world.

How to use?

There is flow between these levels of innovation. People have to try, again and again, to find better ways of doing things. Most of the time, the insight that leads to a new idea is not 'new to this world' and nor is the new idea. Because people are so busy, they may not take the time to find existing solutions that would be as good (or better) than the new idea they just had. The problem with this is that you can spend all your precious innovation time doing what has been done before. Or spending all your innovation money on doing something that isn't even an improvement.

The trick is to understand quickly how the new idea would work *before* spending too much time or money. Then search for alternatives – using your network and the internet. Better to find what you need off-the-shelf than build it made-to-measure. Save your energy for what only you can do because only you – and your people – understand the details of the situation and the desired future.

Key questions

- Has the new idea been tried before? Has someone invented something better? Can you buy what you're thinking of making? Is there a cheaper alternative?
- What will the new idea change? Will it change nothing or change everything? Is the new idea an improvement? Is the new idea a new generation of an existing system? Is the new idea something that can be legally protected?
- How will you build the new system? What help do you need? Who do you need to work with inside your group? Who do you need outside of the group? What has to change for your new idea to work? How dependent or independent is your new idea?

Related ideas

Disruptive innovation doesn't always need to be very new. It may be based on something as straightforward as being willing (and able) to provide fewer features at a cheaper price. Each level of the innovation pyramid offers new opportunities for disrupting existing systems and markets. Each level of the innovation pyramid also offers new capability traps where it is tempting to keep looking for the most complex, less likely source of innovation.

---

case study

Innovation in action

There are nearly 2 million homeless people in the USA – and an estimated 100 million homeless in the rest of the world. In an act of disruptive innovation, Utah decided to give away homes instead of criminalising or persecuting the homeless. Innovators did the maths. They found that providing apartments and social care cost less than providing emergency care and jail cells. Homelessness has decreased by 78% in less than a decade and the state aims to provide homes for all before 2015.

Burgelman and Seigel's minimum winning game

It's good to be ambitious. Innovators like to aim high. Many people are motivated by doing something remarkable, something that matters. Yet it is also important to know what the minimum acceptable result needs to be. Everyone benefits from figuring out the lowest threshold for performance, design or anything else that will shape the future success or failure of the innovation.

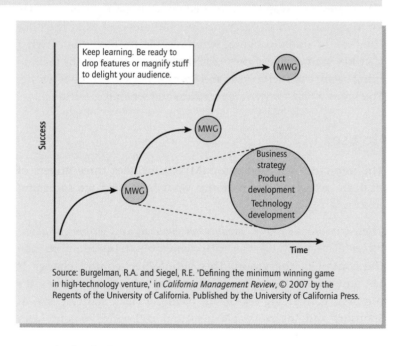

Source: Burgelman, R.A. and Siegel, R.E. 'Defining the minimum winning game in high-technology venture,' in *California Management Review*, © 2007 by the Regents of the University of California. Published by the University of California Press.

Innovator's insights

It's smart to limit your faith in fixed plans but it can be dumb to ignore strategic thinking. The innovator can be so in love with the new ideas that no time is made for strategy. The technologist can be so hands deep in the innards of machines or software that they fail to design what is wanted.

Some level of uncertainty is a fact. But it should not be an excuse for not having a guiding strategy. Customers don't always know exactly what they want. But this is no reason for pretending that they don't exist. Or for making lazy assumptions about how real people think, live and work.

Yes – there is always genius and luck in every successful innovation. But there is still room for strategy and clarity. Who will be using your new idea? In practical terms, what will your product or service have to do before it will be useful and popular? What technology must be developed?

These questions keep effort focused on what has to be done. They avoid over-kill, where everyone does too much of what they like the best, or under-cooking, where people do too little of what they like or understand the least. These questions help the team to bring balance to their efforts and know when something is wrong. You know when something is critical and when it is optional.

How to use?

The minimum winning game (MWG) includes three drivers of strategic action that can clarify what is needed for successful innovation.

There's *business strategy*, *product development* and *technology development*. These will all evolve with elements both inside and outside the control of the group. This out-of-direct-control change is not an excuse for skipping the rigour of strategic thinking – it's the most convincing reason for having a clear, strategic MWG. Sponsors and investors, partners and colleagues benefit from understanding your logic and goals.

Most innovation journeys start without a clear strategy. In part this is because the motivation of the innovator is often not specifically commercial. The innovator may be trying to solve a problem or play with what they enjoy rather than trying to make money.

There is a danger of excessive focus on making the new idea better rather than ever making the most of the new idea. There are sketches on napkins and whiteboards. There are projects and prototypes. There may even be marketing and financial forecasts. There is less often clear thinking about what the innovation must be able to do to become popular enough to survive and then thrive.

If your innovation is successful, there will be a chain of MWGs stretching back to the start of the project. It's useful to have a sense of the minimum to be accomplished every six months, 12 months and 18 months. You may accomplish much more. You will have many other goals and tasks to be completed in each of the three drivers. It is how they come together that shapes success.

Key questions

- Why are we trying to innovate? What is the market for the innovation? What is the existing business strategy? What is the existing strategy around the innovation? What do you have to accomplish in the next six months for your innovation to succeed? What comes next?

- What resources does the innovation need? How can the innovation justify the resources? How can the innovation start to generate its own resources? How will we judge progress between now and then? Have we discovered anything that could get us there early?

- What *must* you do? What doesn't really matter? How can you move effort for what doesn't matter to what does matter? How can you move resources from what is above the MWG to what is below the MWG? What is the next MWG? And the next? How is the MWG evolving?

Related ideas

The minimum winning game is about strategy, while strategy is about shaping the future – or the shortest route to desirable ends with available means. An example of this shortest route approach comes from Garry Newman, who was already a successful game designer when he decided to launch Rust, an online survival game, *before* it was finished. In fact, he describes it as being 90% unfinished, but they delivered it anyway and in just two months there have been one million sales.

case study

Innovation in action

Tesla Motors is the only new US car company to be floated on the public stock exchange since Ford in 1956. It has succeeded where other electric car innovators have failed. Much of its success comes from the adaptable blending of strategy, product and technology. It focused on building a popular car and a profitable business, not just building the technology for a better electric car.

Tesla launched a luxury sports car first to generate interest and revenue from early adopters. It used an existing and established sports car from Lotus to reduce costs while generating greater interest and credibility. It invested savings in a battery-charging infrastructure, necessary for widespread popularity of an electric car, and got the money back through tax and carbon credits.

The company continues to sell its technology to rivals because it creates revenue and moves them towards a dominant design. Tesla chooses to cut back investment when running out of funds. It borrowed money from the government and then paid it back. Any company could have done it, but Tesla continues to take the time and effort to craft each step into a successful strategic journey.

Osborn and Parnes' creative problem-solving (CPS)

Innovation needs ideas. Ideas need to be generated. As an innovator, you are going to need lots of new ideas from time to time. Or lots of different creative alternatives for solving a particular problem when it arises. You want people sharing their craziest ideas so that you can eventually find something worthwhile. You want ideas that will break boundaries and lead to breakthroughs.

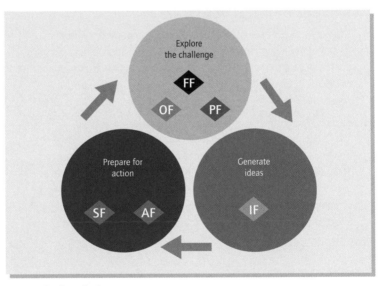

Innovator's insights

Alex Osborn was the slickly dressed, Bronx-born, brainstorming advertising executive who coined the term 'brainstorming'. It was a way of describing the kind of idea generation meetings that he used with his team. He wrote a famous book – *Applied Imagination* – and started to work with a professor, Sidney Parnes, at Buffalo State College. Parnes continued to develop and research effective ways of solving problems creatively for the next half a century.

It's an approach that reminds you, as an innovator, that practical creativity – or innovation – is a process rather than an accident, while also being a process that relies on accidents. Breakthroughs rely on mistakes, unexpected insights, crazy connections – and the production of those mistakes, insights and connections tend to follow a predictable shape.

Be careful. Many people formalise so much that the creativity is squeezed out. There's a danger of over-using the same brainstorming techniques, complete with ice breakers and adhesive notes. Make sure you safeguard the unreasonable passion and unrelenting playfulness on which radical creativity depends. Creativity checklists have great value, if they free energy for deep advances.

How to use?

Stage one is to *explore the challenge*. You do some *objective finding* so that you have a sense of the wish, goal or challenge, dissatisfaction or desire that is driving the search for a creative solution. *Fact finding* allows you to gather data about the situation, people, facts and feelings involved. *Problem finding* is the part where you ask questions about whether the problem is the best problem to solve.

Stage two is to *generate ideas*. It has only one step – *idea finding*. The process of exploring possibilities and insights, connecting existing ideas in new ways, stretching reality to make new dreams possible. Get people building on each other's ideas, making them come to life, combining skills and perspectives to explore the value and expand the practical elements of new ideas.

Stage three is to *prepare for action*. You move towards *solution finding* by building on the ideas that have been generated and exploring criteria for deciding which new ideas to nurture further. You develop the insights into ideas and give your ideas working mechanisms. And then you pursue the tasks and work necessary to transform new ideas into reality with a process of *acceptance finding*.

Key questions

- What problems are you trying to solve? Are you solving the most valuable problems? Are you solving the wrong problem? Who – or what – is driving you to solve the problem? How urgent is the solution? What has been tried before? How well did it succeed? Or fail? Why?

- How can you simplify existing solutions to make them affordable, usable or attractive to solve new problems? Or old problems for new people? What do you do to get the group giddy, relaxed, adventurous, bold, silly, brave, weird, competitive and high?

- Who can help you solve the unsolvable? Who can you bring into your group to inspire the curiosity driven results? How does your idea look as a picture? Or a comic strip? As a cardboard prototype? Or a role play? How do you test the idea before betting big on it?

Related ideas

Revolution tends to happen in a society, argued James Davies, sociologist, when the gap between reality and expectation becomes unacceptable. This is particularly likely to happen when times have been good for long enough to raise expectation, followed by a sudden reversal of fortunes. Similarly, William McKinley, management theorist, shows how when leaders respond with inflexible innovation they tend to enter a downward spiral. If they respond with flexible innovation, they tend to succeed.

case study

Innovation in action

Manu Prakash, bioengineer, explored the challenge of wiping out malaria. He figured out that any solution needed to be able to scale up to help improve the matching of the correct treatment to specific strains of the disease. Correct diagnosis required affordable microscopes. The wild idea was to produce the *foldoscope* – a microscope that is made from a single sheet of folded paper plus rugged inexpensive spherical lenses. The foldoscope can magnify 2,000 times and costs only 50 cents.

Altshuller's theory of inventive problem-solving (TRIZ)

Innovators want both aspects. They don't want to live with compromise. You can find opportunities for valuable innovation by simply looking at unwelcome compromises in existing ideas. You want the product to be high quality *and* low cost. You want the service to be sophisticated *and* easy to use.

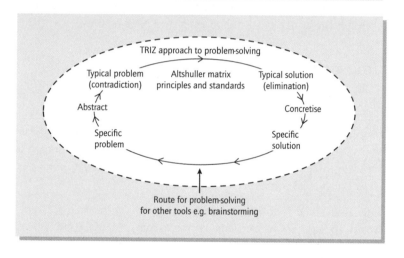

Innovator's insights

When trying to solve a specific problem, it's tempting to just try something and see whether it works. You think of a specific solution and give it a go. You may think it will succeed and then be surprised when it doesn't. Or you may assume that you will have to try, try, try again. This trial-and-error approach can be very, very ineffective because you get stuck in the uniqueness trap. Every attempt is unique, each experiment isolated, overdependent on chance, rather than part of an overall strategy.

You can use this method to get better at creative problem-solving. The approach actually helps you to *solve* problems creatively rather than merely *be* creative while attempting to solve problems. The distinction is valuable. Many organisations want better ways of doing things but don't make the abstract journey to understand better what kind of problem they want to solve. They rely on what they already know, and that makes them slow at finding a smart way to overcoming contradictions.

As a leader of innovation, you can get better at using these tools. You can make sure your people gain training in the principles or the specifics. There are complete lists of contradictions, methods and ways of combining them all. You can also choose to take just the fundamental logic of the approach and ensure that you move between the concrete to the abstract and back again.

How to use?

The trick is to find a contradiction in the existing idea that leads you from a specific problem to a typical problem. Specific problems are unique but they also tend to share similarities with many other problems. If you can match a specific problem to a typical problem then you can use a set of pre-prepared approaches to find a typical solution.

The next stage is to move from the typical solution to a real-world specific solution. This is a creative process that moves from the abstract solution to a concrete solution. The specific solution eliminates the contradiction that was at the root of the problem. You have now made the journey from problem to solution – and along the way you may have created a valuable innovation.

There are a set of methods, effects and tricks in this approach to creative problem-solving. The methods in the original TRIZ approach are worth understanding. Here's a selection of them:

■ *Doing it inversely* is about taking the opposite action. Instead of heating something you cool it. Instead of going up you go down. Instead of adding another feature you take a feature away. You reverse whatever is done in the existing approach. In this way you find new possibilities.

- *Doing it in advance* involves doing something earlier in a process. By changing the order of events, an earlier contradiction is overcome. Putting a saw blade inside a plaster cast allows the plaster cast to be easily cut from inside out. This is simpler and easier than cutting outside in.

- *Doing a little less* means doing something less than is obvious. If you want to reduce the cost of something then do a little less of something that seems vital to your competitors but is of little interest to your customers. If there's no room for a fully inflated tyre, included a deflated tyre.

- *Matryoshka* invites you to place one object inside another in the way that Russian dolls work. You can move weights into the tyres of a vehicle to increase the stability of a moon buggy. You can include a series of new services inside existing services to fix contradictions in what they offer.

Key questions

- What is the specific problem that you are trying to solve? What are the specific contradictions you are trying to overcome? How can you abstract the problem into something that makes the problem dynamic more obvious?

- What typical problem is your specific problem like? How are similar problem types solved? How can you solve the problem on paper? How can you move from abstract solutions to concrete real-world solutions? What contradictions does your concrete solution solve?

- What knowledge could solve your problem easily? How can your group collect knowledge about other inventions and solutions that would help solve problems in the future? Who in your group can become a working expert in TRIZ? How can you solve the impossible?

Related ideas

Insight is about what happens when a problem is no longer straightforward to solve or when obvious solutions are not considered sufficient. *Analogical transfer* can help because it maps a difficult-to-solve problem onto a problem that is already solved. When you find the right analogy, you can experience the 'aha' moment because our brains let us know that they have been successful in selectively encoding, combining and comparing information.

---

case study

Innovation in action

Around 2003, a white cleaning sponge known as the Magic Eraser became very popular because it could get rid of impossible stains – like ink, sticky residue and wax crayons – and because it was non-toxic. It just required light pressure and a little water. Even more amazing was that Magic Eraser was an existing product – melamine foam – used as insulation for more than 20 years. This is an example of ideality – new solutions that are better *and* simpler than old solutions.

Osterwalder's business model canvas

If you have a new insight or new idea for improving something but do nothing with it – then you have not invented or innovated. If you don't share it – the idea will die with you. If you put your insights into practice, they can become innovations. It's important to nurture the original insight with a group until the workings of the new idea – in the real world – is clear enough to take action.

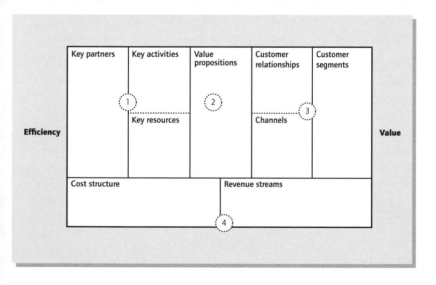

Innovator's insights

The strength of the business model canvas is that it is structured enough to give clarity to discussion while also being flexible enough to adapt to your particular situation. The original author developed the tool as part of his doctoral thesis. He wanted a consistent way of describing a business model. This can encourage mutual understanding between groups and individuals.

For innovators, it is clearer how building blocks can be redesigned, reconfigured or reconnected in new ways to support new ideas. The canvas includes nine blocks divided into four sections labelled *infrastructure* (key activities, key resources, partner network), *offering* (value proposition), *customers* (segments, channels, relationships) and *finances* (cost structure and revenue streams).

How to use?

Photocopy the canvas. Draw it up on a whiteboard. Project it on to a wall. Use it at first to expand your understanding of your existing business – or the way an existing situation works. Use it to flesh out different approaches to reaching out to customers or making a new idea useful. Share it with other people, and discuss changes, adaptations, extensions, possibilities and practicalities.

There are five phases suggested for a formal business model design. *Mobilise* is about helping people to understand the purpose and process. *Understand* gathers the information that will help you to complete the canvas. *Design* generates alternatives that can be tested. *Implement* builds real-world versions of the business models while *manage* modifies the model to make it work. The key, as with all these models, is to use only the parts that help you. The goal for an innovator is not to become an expert in the tool but, instead, to use the tool to explore and then exploit new ideas.

Key questions?

- Does your business model help, or hinder, the value you offer customers? How can you create new ways of working to increase the value customers see in your offer? If you change the way people buy, or pay, for your innovation, will it become more popular – or more profitable?

- What alternatives are there? How can you borrow business models from other industries? Can you get advertisers to pay? Or ask customers? Can people pay as they go – renting or subscribing? How can you reverse the typical split of profit and cost? How do you get fans to pay more/earlier or laggards to pay less/later in the process?

- What do customers really value in what you offer? Or what you could offer? Can you split the value offered into different parts? Can you sell them separately? Can you bundle the value together? Is it better to offer your new idea as part of someone else's offer?

Related ideas?

Business models are just the way businesses work; they describe how value is delivered to the customer and how profits are made for the business. Osterwalder's work was influenced by the concepts proposed by Kim and Mauborgne. And back in 1979, the value chain was proposed by Michael Porter, Harvard professor, and can be used in a very similar way to play creatively with different ways of creating value for customers. Both models are included in *The Strategy Book*.

---

case study

Innovation in action

Several years ago, Disney introduced the FastPass system to allow people to join one virtual queue at a time. It gave them an edge because people really hate wasting their time in line. Disney then dreamt up the Magicband+, a waterproof rubber bracelet that wirelessly identifies the guest and brings together virtual queuing, tickets, restaurant books and hotel keys. One billion dollars – so far – invested in customer experience innovation. Something most businesses would never consider.

Amabile's internal and external motivation

Individual creativity is motivated. Some of the motivation to create is internal. You may love the task for its own sake. You may have the task expertise and find it easy. Or you may have creativity skills that you enjoy putting into action. The external environment also affects creativity motivation. The resources available, interest in your work, and way you're treated. These all impact on creative desire.

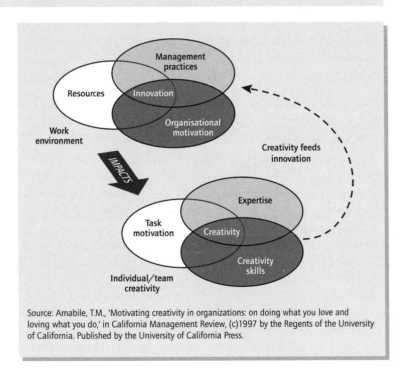

Source: Amabile, T.M., 'Motivating creativity in organizations: on doing what you love and loving what you do,' in California Management Review, (c)1997 by the Regents of the University of California. Published by the University of California Press.

Innovator's insights

The motivation to be creative can be external or internal. You can love being creative and be driven by a deep drive to do creative work. You can also love a particular objective and be driven to be creative by a deep need to achieve that goal. The outside world may encourage or discourage your internal desire to solve problems creatively.

Intrinsic motivation is about how you feel about the task or goal itself. You may find any part of the activity or outcome motivational. You have positive feelings about doing the work. You may be curious, satisfied, challenged or interested. You are engaged with the work.

Extrinsic motivation is about how you feel about something outside the task that changes how you feel about the task. You may like your job but dislike your boss. You may find creativity inspiring but find the goals of your corporation depressing. You may find little pleasure in the task but be motivated to complete it by the rewards that follow. You can love the purpose, not the work.

Some people are more intrinsically motivated. Some are more influenced by extrinsic rewards. Some creativity is discouraged by external judgement and rewards. Dragging a new idea kicking and screaming into the real world needs different kinds of motivation. The best motivation depends on the person, situation, timing and task.

How to use?

Consider what motivates you to do useful work. Some of that is about how effectively you can do the task sufficiently well to gain satisfaction, some is about challenge and some about the task itself. Think about what demotivates you. This might include your working environment, the opinions of others and the available resources to get the job done. Think carefully about the extra demands of being creative. Most people have to be motivated enough to do something that is unknown. There is a risk of the new idea being wasted. There is a gamble of both time, energy and reputation.

Examine the nature of the tasks that you need people to complete. If there is a lot of uncertainty about the success of the work, then you'll need to find the most effective motivation for the people you have. Some people are very, very motivated by the challenge in the task. They need to know that completing the task has bragging-rights. They like knowing that their work is worthwhile.

Some will apply creativity to any task for the right external reward. Others need to know that they are safe before doing anything that is not guaranteed to succeed. You need to find ways of reassuring the performance obsessives that they will be protected if they take risks. Use the model to assess the motivational situation around the kind of innovation you want to see.

Key questions

- Do your people have the skills they need to be creative in their work? Are your processes helpful to new ideas? Do your processes encourage creative problem-solving? Do you make it easy for people to match their intrinsic motivation to the task they work on? Do managers take new ideas away from the people who care most about them?

- What can you do to encourage a pro-creativity social environment? Are new ideas harshly treated when they are shared? Do people waste or disrespect new ideas? Is diversity of people encouraged? How much does politics get in the way of good ideas? How can you get the passions and obsessions of people involved in creating stuff that matters?

Related ideas

Gonshiro Kubota, then 19, started making cast-iron water pipes in 1890s' Osaka. Not long after, his company began making powered heavy equipment. Underlying his philosophy that 'society keeps corporations going forward' the company is still committed to creating 'productive human environments'. Their problem-solving space is a global loop connecting food, water and the environment: establishing reliable water contributes to abundant production of food thus creating comfortable lives for all. The products transform deserts into lush green land hence its slogan 'For Earth, For Life'. The company's sincere problem-solving style motivates people to create useful innovation.

Innovation in action

For innovation, creative spaces help creative thinking – like the Langham Hotel in Melbourne, voted the best hotel in Australia. It has also won awards for its innovative culture, helped by the creation of innovation spaces for every department. Employees managed the completion of their own space for new thinking and collaboration as part of a competition to increase motivation to create new ideas

Guilford's convergent and divergent thinking

Some people are good at learning the correct answer to a question. They may tend to believe that there is only one answer to every question. That approach can make people good at exams but not so good at creativity. Others can see countless possible answers to every question. They may even believe that there are no correct answers. Both convergent and divergent thinking are valuable.

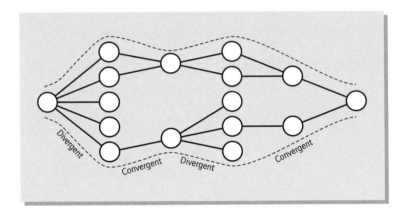

Innovator's insights

Intelligence is not, as many people think, just one kind of ability. For practical creativity, we need lots of mental abilities blended together. Some recognise contents, some organise what is recognised into products, and are able to operate upon those products. We are able to move what we see or learn around in our minds. We can play with ideas, facts and memories.

Convergent thinking is about applying existing forms, recipes and standards. Using what is known may not require very much understanding. Thinking deeply is seldom required because the approach can be applied *without* knowing much – if anything

– about the underlying logic. At the extreme, only one correct answer is expected and accepted. From this perspective, knowledge is fixed.

Divergent thinking rejects fixed formulas. It really wants to understand. It is capable of finding many answers to questions. It is capable of finding many new questions in response to existing questions. Thinking is deep and wide as it makes more new connections from any starting point. At the extreme, there are never any correct answers. From this perspective, knowledge is always fluid.

There is evidence that many people have a bias towards convergence or divergence. The convergent thinkers will tend to focus on the logical, realistic, objective, structured and quantitative. The divergent thinkers are more often intuitive, imaginative, impulsive, holistic and qualitative. To create something new and then make it work, convergent and divergent thinking need to be combined.

How to use?

As an innovator, you need to be a combination thinker able to converge *and* diverge. Any successful innovation effort needs both divergent and convergent thinking at different stages of creative problem-solving. This happens each time you move from a problem to multiple ideas and then back again to choose a more limited set of ideas to explore in detail. If there is nothing but divergence, the likelihood is that there will never be a completed product from all that thinking. If there is nothing but convergence it is unlikely that there will be anything new or better – nothing not already known.

Look for the right kind of balance between divergent and convergent thinkers. There are tests of thinking styles that can help identify both biases. These can introduce another valuable source of diversity into your team or organisation. People who always know the textbook answer need to work along with those who love to tear up the rule book.

There is still a difference between general divergent thinking and divergent thinking specific to a particular problem. Sometimes a complete novice is useful to prompting innovation, but more often expertise must be combined with creativity. Respect hard-won know-how. Use expertise as a tool.

Develop divergent thinking ability. The evidence is people can get better at divergent thinking. Practicing verbal and visual spontaneity can improve the fluency, originality and flexibility of your ideas. You can extend that general divergent thinking skill to the specific kind of issues, problems and goals that matter to you or your organisation. Create more possibilities. And then choose.

Key questions

- How far can you let your mind wander before it gets specific? Does your mind get lost in alternatives for so long that you don't produce anything finished? How many alternative uses can you think of for an item on your desk? How many different ways can you list as being alternatives for whatever strategy, design or plan you are currently following?

- Who are the divergent thinkers in your group? Who are the convergent thinkers? Who are those best combination thinkers? How can you recruit more of the thinkers you need? When will you encourage them to choose between ideas? When will you inspire yet more ideas? How can you build the convergent/divergent flow of thinking into your innovation rhythm?

Related ideas

Between divergence and convergence, there is the ability to spot opportunities. According to Leonie Baldacchino, at Warwick Business School, the intuitive ability of entrepreneurs to identify good opportunities increases with experience. With real-world experience, the entrepreneurial innovator gains *versatile cognitive strategies* to move between analytical thinking and intuition.

case study

Innovation in action

Moving from divergent search to convergent solutions allowed Adidas to see an opportunity in directional energy return. This was originally reported in academic sports research from Darren Stefanyshyn at the University of Calgary and led to experimentation with designs and filing of patents for innovative running shoes. Six years later, Adidas' head of innovation announced two new shoes: Bounce, followed by Switchblade. Adidas has bet on a future of what they call energy running.

Ries' build-measure-learn wheel

You want to find out whether a new idea is the right idea for you. The smart thing to do is quickly build some kind of working prototype and put it to work. By measuring what happens, you can reach a decision about whether to continue, change or cancel your work on the new idea.

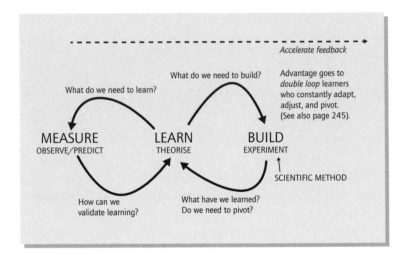

Accelerate feedback

What do we need to build?

What do we need to learn?

Advantage goes to *double loop* learners who constantly adapt, adjust, and pivot. (See also page 245).

MEASURE
OBSERVE/PREDICT

LEARN
THEORISE

BUILD
EXPERIMENT

SCIENTIFIC METHOD

How can we validate learning?

What have we learned? Do we need to pivot?

Innovator's insights

As an innovator, you have new ideas, but don't know what will succeed or fail. You want to learn rapidly what works and what doesn't. You need a rapid learning process between new ideas, what is built, measured and learnt and the decision to pivot or preserve. Thinking like a scientist helps.

The build-measure-learn wheel is part of moving from (the unknown value) of a new idea to the (known value) of a successful institution. The new idea can become part of an existing organisation, business, process or society. Or, a new organisation, business, process or society can be built around it. The point here is that a new idea needs to adapt until it can thrive over the long term.

To thrive over the long term, the new idea starts by getting people motivated enough to support it with time and money. You will usually need to measure progress and decide on priorities. But you also have to avoid the pitfalls of standard accounting approaches. Innovation accounting establishes a baseline – perhaps a competitor's product, or a prototype. Use the baseline to test assumptions.

If the baseline gives you encouragement, you can start playing with your prototype, or tuning the engine, making modifications that provide more data, more learning, until you have enough to make longer-term decisions about whether to stop working, change the business model or invest. The decision to invest more effort into your new idea – or start-up – is not the end, but the start of another cycle of experimentation. This constant innovation can work for organisations of any size.

How to use?

Draw the build-measure-learn wheel up on a whiteboard. The aim is to keep accelerating the feedback loop. You want to learn faster than the situation is changing. So fast that you can see an opportunity, test that opportunity and then adapt to make the most of that opportunity. This is done by building a minimum viable product – or MVP.

Experiment with the response to what you have produced. Using *split tests,* you can offer multiple versions to the same group of customers or different versions to different markets. This can be done very loudly – 'Hey world, which one do you like best?' – or very quietly. Either way, you collect data to allow you to learn. Explore tools and methods of continual improvement to refine, adapt and tune.

Ask questions until you find the root causes of what did or didn't work. Learning is about doing more of what worked and less of what didn't. Be open to possibilities you didn't think of when the original project – or business – started. There might be something better that can be put together with the people, talent, resources and – most importantly – the knowledge that you have gained.

Key questions

- How can you create an innovation sandbox, or island of freedom, somewhere safe for innovators to test their dangerous ideas? Is your culture about working hard doing tasks or about learning fast doing experiments?
- What parts of your organisation can be reshaped to better work with innovation? If innovation accounting is useful, how about innovation recruitment? Innovation appraisals? Innovation risk management? How can you build the value of experimentation into the working day-to-day?
- Why do you think your new idea will succeed? How can you test the hypotheses underlying different parts of your idea? How can you compare your new idea to existing ideas? How can you move beyond pseudoscience to a scientific approach? How can more people get involved?

Related ideas

We use different labels for similar processes of adaptation. The build-measure-learn wheel happily admits its debt to the work of John Boyd, military strategist. You can read about the original at the back of the innovator's toolkit. The RUN loop, described in *Adaptability*, one of my previous books, is another such method which involves three steps: understanding the adaptation required, understanding the necessary adaptation, and necessary adaptation. The goal is fast learning.

case study

Innovation in action

For innovation, you can feed creativity with problems that need to be solved – like two young entrepreneurs in India who wanted to help reduce economic stress and suicide among farmers. Ankit Singh and Vaibhav Tidke invented a patented food dehydrator that uses solar power to dry foods like ginger and Indian gooseberries ready for a more lucrative urban market. It costs five times less than alternatives and pays back famers in 100 days. The aim is one million farmers by 2020.

Shaping better
futures

Christensen's disruptive innovation

As ideas develop, they tend to become more complex. New features are added. Some are valuable to the makers. Some are valuable to a smaller and smaller group of users. Other new additions may not be useful or valuable but are simply thrown into the mix. At the same time, as the value in the new idea becomes less new, it becomes less difficult to copy. This is an opportunity and a threat.

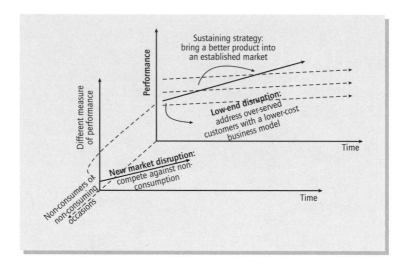

Innovator's insight

Understanding the room for disruption is useful whether you are trying to disrupt an existing situation (to your advantage) or defending an existing situation (to your advantage). The logic is straightforward. Over time, more and more features are added to new ideas.

At some point, the new idea (which may be a product or a service or anything else) becomes overloaded with new additions. It offers too much. And only a small group of people want everything it offers but often everyone has to pay – or buy – the whole package. New additions may be added to justify someone's job, to keep people interested, or simply for no good reason at all.

This process creates opportunities at the low end for someone to produce a new idea, or innovation, that gives people what they really value at a much lower price. There are plenty of people who don't need all the features and don't want to pay for features they don't need. The makers of the original innovation (product, service or anything else) tend to keep focusing on the high end with high prices.

How to use?

You can take the disruptor role. Decide who (or what) you think is the biggest player in a particular area. This might be a brand or a product or a service or an idea. You want to find what dominates either in design (the most popular design) or in usage. And then figure out what you could offer that would push the dominant player out of the space.

You could take the role of the dominant player – or someone already following the dominant design. Think about what kind of offer could be made by a disruptor. They could offer less than you can for a significantly lower price. They could strip out complexity and charge a lower *or* higher price. They could focus on particular parts of the idea and make it much more interesting or useful.

The traditional disruptor stays at the low end which encourages the original innovator to move towards the high end to protect their position. It seems nothing much to give up some low-margin business until the disruptor moves to take over the middle ground and then eventually the high end.

There are many other kinds of disruption possible. People are willing to pay more (or invest more) for a new innovation that is simpler to use. People are also willing to switch to a new innovation that focuses on the particular part of the function that they find most attractive. There is no reason that the disruptive innovation needs to be inferior to the original innovation. It can be much better.

Key questions

- What do you offer that people don't really value? Do new additions make your innovation harder to use? When will you reach value saturation point? How could you offer something at the lower end to appeal to people who don't want to pay for what they don't use?

- What does the market leader offer that people value? What does the market leader offer that people don't really value? Where can your innovation squeeze market leader margins? What part of the market will the leader give up if pushed? How can you deliver the same value for less money? How can you offer increased value by focusing on just one feature?

Related ideas

Disruptive innovation theory didn't start or end with Clayton Christensen. Back in the 1940s, Schumpeter introduced *creative destruction* (see page xxiii) followed in the 1980s by Richard Foster's reports on *s-curve discontinuities* and the *attacker's advantage*. Rebecca Henderson, over at MIT, and Kim Clark, at Harvard, proposed a theory around *radical innovation*. And Geoffrey Moore published his ideas on the innovation chasm. All before Christensen's publication of *The Innovator's Dilemma* in 1992.

---

case study

Innovation in action

Successful disruptors give people what they want, without the crap, which is why their solutions become popular even if they operate in a grey market of contested legality. Internet radio, like Pandora, may ignore or avoid traditional legal frameworks so is attacked by nervous broadcasters. The officially endorsed alternative is DAB (digital audio broadcasting) but sound quality is poor, equipment expensive and innovation slow. The grey market is a great predictor of the future.

Schroeder's innovation journey

Innovation is a journey into the unknown. The smart innovator accepts that the path cannot be known before it is has been made. The good news is that there is a general shape of innovation that can help you figure out how best to prepare and act more powerfully.

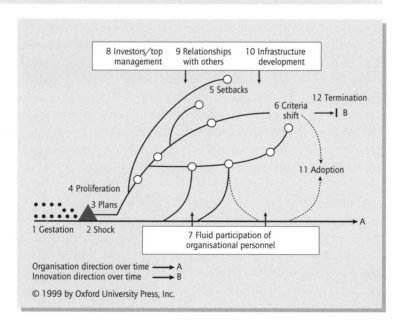

Innovator's insights

Innovation comes from somewhere and goes someplace. The challenge is that it's seldom easy to see where a new idea starts, where it's going to go next or if it will ever stop developing. The path to innovation is not really linear, but nor is it completely random. All innovation moves from (relative) chaos to (relative) order so it helps the innovator to recognise the patterns before they happen.

Initiation

This model was based on a detailed study of many different innovation projects. It showed that there is usually (1) a gestation period that lasts several years (or months or centuries). Eventually you experience (2) a shock to the system that provokes specific efforts to innovate. Not all shocks lead to efforts to innovate, and not all (3) plans to innovate lead to successful innovation.

Development

As soon as serious work on innovation begins, the number of different ways of working on the innovation problem increases. This (4) proliferation creates many divergent, convergent, competing and complementary pieces of work. Because you don't know the exact formula for innovation, you will face (5) setbacks. The (6) criteria for successful innovation will change as you face struggles for power and competitors. People will (7) jump in and out of innovation efforts as external forces, including (8) investors (9) partners and (10) infrastructure, interact.

Implementation

Getting your idea out into the real world happens while you're developing the idea (and even before). Eventually you need to increase the number of people (11) adopting your new idea. The truth is that usually the innovation is never really finished but efforts to innovate will often (12) terminate when resources run out or commitment slows down.

How to use?

Think about where you are on the innovation journey. Usually there are many different stages for different ideas at the same time. Smart innovators get better at understanding where they are, what has happened and what kind of thing is likely to happen next. The innovation journey reminds you that innovation isn't just a neat progression from idea to success.

Show the innovation journey to your team. Write it up on the wall. Find out where everyone thinks you are and where the group wants to travel. Look at the way that each stage presents risks and opportunities for making progress. Don't use it as a detailed step-by-step roadmap. You can't just turn the journey into a project plan. The idea here is to understand the pattern and flow of events.

Key questions

▦ Where did your new idea come from? What was the period of gestation? What kind of ideas came before this one? What happened to them? Did previous ideas succeed or fail? What (shock) led to the decision to try and make this new idea work in the real world?

▦ Who will judge the success of the innovation efforts? How many different opinions are there about the success criteria? How will you deal with the changing people in your group? What can you do to ensure enough engagement when people are temporary? Have you accepted the high probability of setbacks? Will your efforts lead to more innovation cycles? What happens next?

Related ideas

Not everyone on the innovation journey will feel motivated all of the time. The day-to-day grind of doing what has never been done can be emotionally exhausting. Haruko Obokata led research that found a much easier method for creating stem cells that can be grown into many different kinds of cells. She explained how sometimes she wanted to give up but 'encouraged herself to hold on just for one more day'. To cheer herself up, she painted the lab wall pink and yellow, brought in her favourite sofa and decorated the place with Moomin collectibles and stickers.

case study

Innovation in action

Creativity at BRF-Brasil Foods kicked into gear after a liquidity crisis forced the aristocratic owners to sell the company to investors. They needed innovation to drive the transformation and growth of the company. It wasn't a case of having one creative obsessive with the idea of the century but instead a large group of people who needed to kick-start idea-fuelled success. There is now an £58 million innovation centre in São Paulo state with laboratories, experimental kitchens and mini-factories. And the company has gone from around 10 new products each year to over 200 annually.

Usher's path of cumulative synthesis

Ideas come from the minds of individuals. The history of innovation is also the history of the people who create and use – or don't use – those new ideas. Some innovation is the result of people trying to solve a problem or improve a situation. Some innovation comes as the result of insights gained from *doing* something and simply seeing new ways of doing. This path to innovation is natural to us.

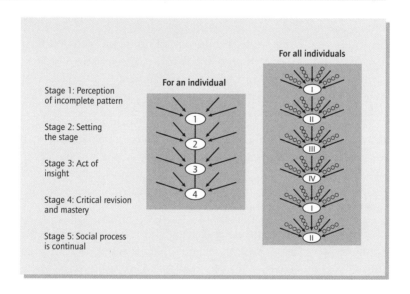

Stage 1: Perception of incomplete pattern

Stage 2: Setting the stage

Stage 3: Act of insight

Stage 4: Critical revision and mastery

Stage 5: Social process is continual

For an individual

For all individuals

Innovator's insights

The **transcendentalist** approach views innovation as coming from miraculous intuition to rare genius. Yet, while the path to creativity includes unplanned events, innovation is never an accident. The **mechanistic** approach argues that innovation is a predictable, gradual process but this is rare.

Cumulative synthesis combines both approaches. Innovation needs accumulated knowledge. We create new ideas with old ideas with acts of individual insight. And individual insights only happen when you understand the problem and have the knowledge to go beyond previous solutions.

Acts of skill are learned. Acts of insight are gained by being in the right place at the right time and seeing gaps and new, better patterns. First you perceive the problem, then set the stage for finding a solution. Eventually a moment of insight allows you to sense a breakthrough. And then critical revision of the new idea until new moments of insight or a finished innovation emerges.

How to use?

New ideas start with some recognition of an incomplete pattern. This is about noticing that there is something missing or that something would be improved if something was changed. You may be asked to focus on filling a gap by someone else who saw it first. You may have seen the gap yourself.

If you want to contribute an innovation, you can deliberately *look* for incomplete patterns. You can move the pieces of a situation or machine or system. Playing with how the pieces fit together can be done in your head. Your imagination can rotate and explore until it sees things as they could be.

Seeing an existing pattern as it could be is an act of insight. Sometimes you'll know pretty much where it came from in your thinking process. Other times it will seem like a mystery – the classic 'aha' moment – even though the thoughts came from somewhere. You have seen a better pattern.

The insight isn't the end of the process because suddenly feeling that there *is* a new (better) pattern is not the same as seeing all the details clearly. It can feel a little like waking up from a vivid dream. You know what you saw and felt but pretty soon the details become harder to pinpoint.

You will have to play around with the new pattern until you can see the way it works – or would have to work in the real world. You will probably go through many cycles. You will move from incomplete patterns and through to eventual mastery of the new pattern. You will start to be able to explain it to others and make it work.

Getting people involved is partly about showing them the new (better) pattern. In this way they can help to support the transformation from how things are to how you want them to be. The social part of creativity is also about combining streams of insights and new patterns from other people.

Key questions

- Are you close enough to the problem? Do you have the skills necessary to find breakthroughs? Have you learned enough to apply that new knowledge in new ways? Who might know what you need to know before a valuable enough problem is discovered? How can you find better problems? Have you obsessed for long enough?

- What gaps are there between how things work and how they could work? Who is already working on the problem? What insights led to previous innovations? How can you extend your knowledge into areas that may prompt insight?

- Are you too close to the problem? What happens if you move away from the problem to see new perspectives? When did you last spend time playing with something that had nothing to do with your job, problem or creative obsession? Where is your next insight hiding?

Related ideas

Wolfgang Köhler was a psychologist who contributed to the Gestalt view that components of the mind can only be understood as part of the whole system of the brain. His most famous experiments showed that trial and error was not sufficient to explain how chimpanzees managed to reach bananas placed out of their reach. A recent review of advances in neuroscience suggests that the *insightful brain* is a complex set of interactions between many different neural structures. In a similar way, innovation arises from a complex set of individual and collection actions.

Innovation in action

There is often a missing link between existing ideas and existing problems. Zoltan Takats, a surgeon, invented the iKnife from 100-year-old electrosurgical technology that uses heat to cut through tissue. He connected an electrosurgical knife and a spectrometer to identify cancerous cells from smoke. The surgeon stops cutting when the knife signals it has reached flesh without any cancer.

Benyus' biomimicry design lens

Nature is good at innovation, so it makes sense to look to nature for innovation. You can start with a specific challenge and then discover how biology has solved similar problems. Or you can immerse yourself in biology and then apply what you learn to real world opportunities. Either way, there is power in plugging your creativity into the mass experiments of nature's laboratory.

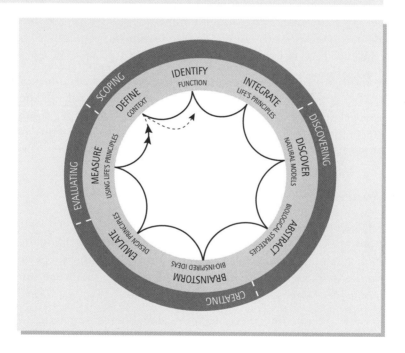

Innovator's insights

It's smart to look beyond what you already know. One way of doing this is by experimenting, but even fast paced trial-and-error can take a very long time. And you will be limited to months or a short number of years rather than the accumulated knowledge that can be discovered from four billion years of life on earth. The shape of a wing, the structure of a termite nest. All offer lessons.

In some ways, this is not new. Humans have borrowed from nature directly, using bones for tools, feathers for quills and fur for clothing, and indirectly; fish suggested flippers while birds gave us our ideas about flight. Da Vinci modelled his flying prototype on bats. Famously, Velcro was inspired by hooks in cockleburs that stuck to the fur of the inventor's dog.

The term 'biomimicry' was popularised by Janine Benyus, a science writer, who later founded the Biomimicry Institute. Again it is really part of an informal movement that includes bionics, bio-inspired engineering and biomimetics – developed in the 1950s by Otto Herbert Schmitt, the pioneering bio-engineer. He is considered the father of the bioengineering approach to design.

You need to discover how something in the natural world works, particularly if it works better than the existing manmade equivalent. Find solutions that are stronger, faster, lighter, more efficient, and less damaging. Understand the inner mechanisms of the biology that is better; and then copy.

How to use?

The biomimicry design spiral, and its equivalent the design lens, can work in two main ways. You can start with understanding the biology and then find a design opportunity. We'll focus, below, on the second approach, beginning with a specific challenge and looking for better solutions in biology.

Start by abandoning preconceptions about what you want to design and instead focus on what you want your design to do. Function comes *before* form because then you can look for how nature does what you want to do. You can look for animals that thrive in environments that are relevant or have abilities similar to those you want in your design. Translate – or biologise – your objectives.

Move outside either physically or mentally. Discover natural models. Look at plant and animal life in its natural habitat. Make notes and sketch movement. Be inspired by the many examples online and in books. Meet with biologists and with others who are attempting the bio-design journey.

Then start to emulate nature in your design efforts. With your head full of biology, use various brainstorming and other creativity techniques to find new, biologically inspired, solutions. This can be done at a relatively shallow, or a profoundly deep level. You can become as expert as you wish. You can go through the design loop as many times as necessary to produce real innovation.

Key questions

▪ What are you really trying to accomplish? What do you want your design to do? What do you want your design to do better? Are you open to function ahead of traditional form?

▪ To what extent is your design in harmony with principles of biomimicry? Does it run on sunlight? Does it use only the energy it needs? Does it fit form to function? Does it recycle everything? Does it reward cooperation? Does it bank on diversity? Is it local? Does it respect the power of limits to avoid damaging our natural and social world?

▪ How does nature do what you want to do? Can you copy the way nature works? Has anyone else tried to copy the way nature works? Can you learn from them?

▪ Who can be your guide to biology? Hire one. How can you spend more time outside? How can you introduce your team to biological approaches to design and innovation? Pin up ideas and photos to inspire yourself and others. Use the biomimetics and biomimicry websites.

Related ideas

Bionics is a similar approach in bioengineering that tends to lead to mechanical solutions that still emulate the movement or function found in nature. It is particularly linked to robots including those that walk like humans, crawl like spiders or swim like dolphins. Or the micro robots designed by six European universities, that mimic the movement of earthworms. Professor Julian Vincent, of Bath University, estimates only 12% of existing technology is based on natural mechanisms, with immense opportunities to discover remarkable new designs to enlighten our innovation efforts.

Do this now!

Recent breakthrough from biomimicry are many, varied and wonderful. The design of tougher ceramics, by scientists from the Université de Lyon, who based their design on mother-of-pearl – or nacre – the shell of a mollusc. Careful study of the water-resistant lotus leaf under electron microscopes has led to designs for self-cleaning fabrics. And even a NASA spacesuit based on the scales of fish and reptiles to allow easy movement in harsh environments of space exploration.

Van de Ven's leadership rhythms

Innovation needs different kinds of leadership at different times. Sometimes it needs someone to obsess about the idea and making it work in the real world. Sometimes it needs someone to invest in the idea and introduce it to new friends. Other times, a new idea needs protection or a critic.

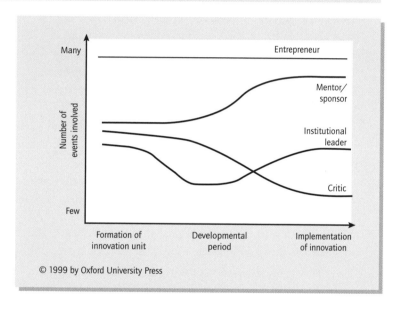

© 1999 by Oxford University Press

Innovator's insights

Look at the traditional stages of a new idea moving from formation, through development and into implementation. Each of these stages will involve different leadership roles to keep the new idea progressing and to make judgements about how new ideas should best develop. Many attempts at innovation use just one or two leadership roles. This is a mistake. There are many:

■ The *entrepreneurial* role is about being the lead obsessive. We're not talking about a business owner but someone who believes in the project, inspiring others to join and pushing it forward. The entrepreneurial role doesn't have all the resources or the political power necessary to make the idea successful but they are going to be doing most of the day-to-day leading and decision-making.

- The *sponsor* takes the lead role of resource hunter. This role is about gaining, or giving, the investment needed for the new idea to thrive. The sponsor role doesn't have as much personal obsession with the new idea but it is about finding the money, recruiting people with time and skills and finding friends for the idea along the journey.

- The *mentor* offers advice and coaching to others along the journey. This role reaches out with expertise gained on other innovation efforts. The mentor role isn't formally involved in finding resources or driving forward the innovation day to day, but it is about preparing the entrepreneur for challenges, sharing solutions, emotional support and a sounding board.

- The *institution* sets the structure and context for the innovation group. This role represents the organisation in a formal way because someone has to make final decisions. The institution isn't so much about backing specific new ideas but it is about settling disputes, protecting the health of the organisation, and giving some kind of institutional viewpoint.

- The *critic* encourages deep thinking about alternatives and consequences. This role represents reality because the new idea only exists in the minds of the people involved. No-one knows whether the new idea will work or what will happen when it is introduced into the real world. It's useful to have deliberate thinking about the good, bad and ugly of the new idea to ensure that the worst is avoided and the best opportunities are grasped.

How to use?

Each of these roles is more, or less, involved at different times. The entrepreneur is involved almost all the time even if there are many other people doing and organising the work.

The sponsor is involved increasingly through the project but not so soon that new ideas are rejected (or invested in too heavily) before they are explored. The new idea will need resources although it is usually better if early resources are accessible more informally. The institution is also involved early on but then moves to allow the new idea to develop before returning later to make final decisions.

The mentor tends to be involved more as the idea gets closer to completion and stays close to the team in a flexible way. The critic needs to be involved early enough in the project to identify fatal flaws and glorious opportunities. Ideally, each role is much more fluid than is traditional.

Key questions

▓ What is your key innovation role? What innovation role do you want next? Or eventually? How can you better develop your experience with different innovation roles?

▓ How well do you fulfil your existing role? How well would members of your team believe that you supported their innovation objectives? Do you understand the perspective of other people playing different roles?

▓ Have you got someone fulfilling each of the roles necessary to innovation leadership? Do you need to recruit someone else? Or someone better? Does everyone know why they are part of the team?

Related ideas

The various roles of innovation are not limited to the list above, and they're not necessarily about one person fulfilling each role in a formal, permanent way. The family owners of Elan Hair Design in Scotland made the decision together to become the world's most eco-friendly hair salon by asking: can we make it green? They recycle harmful aluminium foils, colour tubes and installed solar panels and carbon-neutral furniture. Hair waste is collected and turned into environmentally friendly compost for local farmers. Innovation can start from simple, powerful questions. What is yours?

---

case study

Innovation in action

Faced with disappointing sales in India, Gillette's local brand manager started to collaborate with his counterpart in Singapore. They worked as a team to refocus efforts on frugal innovation – or *jugaad* – to simplify their razors by taking out high-cost features. Acting together as entrepreneurs, they changed the product and launched the 'Shave India Movement' which featured women encouraging their men to shave off stubble, moustaches and beards. Everyone played a different role in challenging what didn't work and then localising the razor for growth in a new market.

Friend's three types of uncertainty

All innovation faces uncertainty, but not all kinds of uncertainty are the same. When you're figuring out what to do next, you will face different levels of the unknown. Sometimes things seem pretty clear because you have been given objectives, know your situation and have made decisions. Other times, you'll barely know where to start. The trick is to understand rather than ignore uncertainty.

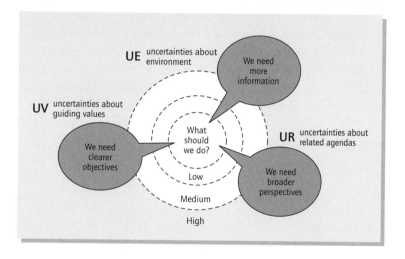

Innovator's insights

Too much uncertainty makes it hard to decide what to do next with innovation. Uncertainty levels can be very high, almost random and certainly chaotic. But sometimes uncertainty just *appears* to be high because you just don't know enough about the situation.

■ *Uncertain environments* are all about the things you don't know yet about the situation. It could be the situation where you'll be trying to use your new idea. Or the situation where you want to sell your idea. Either way, the initial answer to uncertain environments is more research. Find out more. Get more facts. And also more about *how* the environment works.

- *Uncertain related agendas* are about decisions linked to your new idea. Your innovation may be highly dependent on decisions that you don't know. It makes sense to find out which are the decisions so that you know when to innovate, when to wait and who (or what to influence). Take a broader view. Look at the bigger picture. Connect the decision chain in your favour.

- *Uncertain values* is all about not knowing the guiding objectives for your innovation. This might be tastes, preferences or needs that will shape the likely popularity of your new idea in the real world. It might also be the guiding opinions and values *inside* your group. Explore the objectives of your innovation. Clarify what people value. Identify differences of opinion.

How to use?

Some people pretend there is no uncertainty and that everything is under control. Other people act as though everything is uncertain, so there is no point trying to reduce uncertainty. In the real world, uncertainty levels can be reduced by finding out enough about what could affect the new idea.

Key questions

- What don't you know? What's stopping you knowing what to do next? What kind of information is missing? How can you plug the knowledge gaps that are preventing effective action? How can you make the innovative path more attractive by plugging those uncertainty gaps?

- Do you know enough about related decisions? Who can guide you through what else might affect your new idea? How do you find out the chain of events that would lead to the success of your new idea? What is needed to get support? What is needed to get approval? Or adoption?

Related ideas

There are always unknowns with every new idea. Yet it makes sense to reduce those unknowns where possible. Just 90 seconds of research can be all it takes to find out that your new idea has already been turned into a useful innovation by someone else. To be a novice may be useful but some gaps in knowledge will just mean that your innovation either doesn't work or isn't really new at all.

---

case study

Innovation in action

Underground restaurants – also known as supper clubs – have sprung up all over the world. From Charlie's Burger, a series of temporary, secret restaurants in Canada, to Prêt-a-Diner in Berlin that uses roller rinks for mystery meals. For some people, they are about sharing the costs of an open invitation dinner party. For others, supper clubs allow entrepreneurial chefs to experiment before paying licensing fees, greasing palms and meeting the demands of bureaucratic regulations.

Teece's win, lose, follow, innovate grid

Some people make new ideas useful. Others make new ideas profitable. The person who first invents something new is often not the person who becomes the most famous inventor. Just as the company who is first to market with a new innovation may not become the market leader. As an innovator, it is valuable to know the difference between winning, losing, following and innovating.

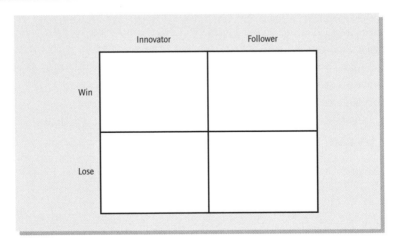

Innovator's insights

It is possible to be first and fail. It is equally possible to be second and succeed. Or third. Or fifty-third. To those who have invested heavily in being the innovator, it is hard to accept that someone else will profit from your investment. Those who fail (or are less successful) are often tempted to label those who succeed (or are more successful) as imitators who only copy. This is a mistake.

Appropriability regime is about how easy (or hard) it is to protect the profit from an innovation. Some legal systems will protect some kinds of ideas and make it easier to be paid if they are used. Some innovations are also hard to copy. This may be because the skills are difficult to acquire. It may also be because you are able to keep the details of the idea secret.

Dominant design is about whether your innovation becomes the most popular way of doing things. There are many ways of doing (almost) anything. Some ideas become more popular than others. Some ways become more (or less) profitable than others. The dominant design does not have to be the best way of doing something. Circumstances determine which ideas succeed. And which fail.

Complementary assets are what is needed to make the new idea work. Complementary assets are also about what is needed to profit from the new idea. Your big new idea must be made useful not only once but many times. You have to be able to make the idea of a car work in the real world. Then you have to be able to make the idea of mass production successful. And then you have to market the idea better than the next manufacturer. And manage costs. And make cars people want.

How to use?

Accept that there is a difference between winning, losing, innovating and copying. This is already hugely valuable because you are less likely to become bitter when someone else appears to be successful copying your new idea. You are also less likely to become passive (stuck) when someone appears to have got to the market first with an idea. With innovation it is always the beginning.

Think of examples for each of the boxes. Find some winning innovators, like Philips with the CD or Pilkington with Activ self-cleaning glass. Identify some winning followers – think of Apple with the iPod or Beat with headphones. Jot down an example of a losing follower, some company who was late to the game, in the same way as HP was with the slate tablet. Then add a losing innovator – someone who lost despite being first, as with Nintendo's Wii U, Nokia or Palm with the smartphone.

You will find that rarely – if ever – is the first to have an idea the one who wins biggest with the new idea. In part, that's because no idea is ever perfect or complete. This means that what appears first is not necessarily ready to be successful. This can be because it is missing some vital ingredient. A particular version of a new idea can also arrive too early to be popular. Timing is almost everything.

Consider innovations in your arena or market. Consider the appropriability regime and whether existing innovations are well enough protected. Think about whether your own innovations are protected. Figure out how you might patent or copyright your new idea – even if you want to make it freely available. Look for innovations to copy and then improve. That's also innovation.

Key questions

- What dominant designs are there in your market or area of interest? What has to be included as part of any innovation? Are you sure it has to be included? Can you go beyond the current accepted standard? Can you create a standard around your innovation?

- How will you protect your idea? Can your idea be legally protected? Can the recipe for your idea be kept secret? Can your way of doing things be made so distinctive that it can't be copied? Can openly sharing your new idea be more profitable than hiding your idea?

- What does the new idea need? Is there a reason that the new idea hasn't yet succeeded? Have you got complementary assets that help you make the innovation more successful? Can you figure out innovations that complement skills or resources you already have?

Related ideas

A beautiful idea is never perfect. This means that there is always the possibility of further improvement and innovation. Some people are discouraged when they realise that someone else has already had a similar idea, but the smart innovator often feels pleased because they can start work on a version of the idea that is more useful or more usable. Look for gaps, look for friction, listen to complaints, read reviews, keep what people love and subtract what people hate.

case study

Innovation in action

Entrepreneur Chaleo Yoovidhya invented Red Bull and became the third richest man in Thailand. When jet-lagged marketer Dietrich Mateschitz experienced its famous caffeine and taurine boost, the two men went into business together. Red Bull established a dominant design and created a huge market. It protected its share of that market in two ways. First, via patents for branding – like the blue stripe and the pull-tab with a cut-out logo. Second, by investing 30% of profits in sponsoring extreme sports to appeal most to those who want to go faster. Red Bull can charge double the price for the easy-to-copy drink because it has an impossible-to-copy brand image.

d.school's design thinking modes

There's making a new idea work, and then there's making a new idea work properly. You can also try to make a new idea work effectively, or beautifully. If you apply enough creativity to the opportunity you may even be able to shape the meaning around your new idea so that people *feel* better.

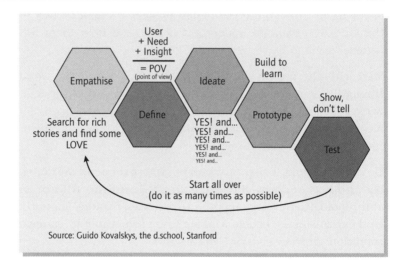

Source: Guido Kovalskys, the d.school, Stanford

Innovator's insights

If your innovation is more problematic than the problem, that's a problem. Or stated in another way, your new idea must lead to greater opportunities, and a better future, if it is to be worthwhile. That doesn't have to happen immediately but eventually, you need to bring together what is feasible, what is desirable, and what is viable into a design that is far less costly than the benefit gained.

Design thinking as a movement aims to improve the way innovation is done. Part of this is increasing **empathy** for those who will be using your innovation by putting people at the heart of your innovation efforts – making it human-centred. The other part is an emphasis on **rapid prototyping** – you make stuff to find your way to the stuff you want to make – it's a hands on approach.

How to use?

Print the diagram out. Or just draw it up on a whiteboard. Design thinking is highly visual and it will help to get people thinking visually from the start. Use permanent pens, if you dare, for the main modes. Use whiteboard pens to add annotation. This isn't about going through a linear design process, it's about a way of thinking. You want to understand people and help them feel better.

Start with the people you're trying to help. Look at the world through their eyes. Learn more about their way of life, mode of work, beliefs and values. Thinking like a human-centred designer means **adopting a beginner's mind-set**. Set aside judgement. Seek patterns and really listen.

Go into the world. Video and observe. Ask what people are doing, but also how *and* why they are doing it. Learn the skills of an anthropologist. Develop rapport. Evoke stories. Explore emotions. Find extreme users, people who are using something in extreme conditions or in new ways. Gain insights.

Next you want to test your insights. Work with your group to share and capture stories. Look for patterns and find themes that can be built up – or synthesised – into something testable. Unpack what you have gathered into a simple quadrant with boxes for what people say, do, think and feel.

Develop prototypes that turn your insights into something more testable. Prototypes can be made of physical bits and pieces, cardboard, play dough, Lego, words, electronics or paper. They can increase empathy, test mechanisms, work with users, or help reach decisions about what ideas to pursue.

Key questions

- What do your users like? What do they wish? What do they want if there were no constraints? Use these three questions to develop How-Might-We (HMW) statements from the point-of-view (POV) of your users.

- Have you developed insights that are meaningful, actionable and focused? What's the point of your insight? Who says it matters? What's new about your insight? Who will care if you make it work?

- What do people think and feel about your prototype? What do they like? Or want to see more of? What do they want to change? What do they hate? Where is there enthusiasm even where there is a lack of quality? What questions still need to be answered?

Related ideas

Fleming, professor of Organizational Behaviour at Berkeley, argues that breakthrough ideas are often the result of multidisciplinary efforts. People share knowledge that takes the whole group to the edge of what is known. These efforts are hard work because of the cycles of learning required on all sides. They produce fewer ideas for improvement but – and this is vital – they produce much more powerful breakthrough innovations.

Do this now!

For innovation, remember that it is valuable to teach creativity skills that can be developed as any other ability – like Intuit, the software company, who support creativity training with mentoring. Their network of mentors known as innovation catalyst has grown from just 10 in 2009 to more than 200 over 5 years. The role of the mentor is to pass on enthusiasm and working knowledge of deep customer empathy, idea generation from broad to narrow and rapid real world experiments.

Sharing beautiful
ideas

Henderson and Clark's four types of innovation

Some innovation is radical. Big-bang ideas that are different in big impact ways. Some innovation is incremental. Small advances over previous ideas or improvements that don't really change the way you did things previously. But radical changes in one area can lead to little impact in another. And what seems like an incremental innovation can have unexpectedly radical results in the real world.

	Core concepts	
	Reinforced	Overturned
Unchanged	Incremental innovation	Modular innovation
Changed	Architecctural innovation	Radical innovation

Linkages between core concepts and components

Innovator's insights

You may have noticed that some radical innovations have very little impact on the success of the people who made them work. It is also often the case that relatively small innovations have a hugely disruptive impact. And sometimes the existing leader in a particular field fails to make the most of innovation even though it appeared to have the necessary technical skills.

Some of the knowledge necessary for high-impact innovation is about the components involved in the product, machine or technology itself. This knowledge of components is useful but not sufficient for radical innovation. You also need to understand how key concepts regarding particular components are linked together. Radical innovation involves both kinds of knowledge.

Incremental innovations reinforce existing core concepts and leave linkages between those concepts unchanged. It is possible to improve core components with or without leading to any overall improvement. It depends on whether the system has spare capacity for improvement.

Modular innovations overturn previous links between concepts without changing existing concepts. The approach to individual components is new but how they fit together is not new.

Architectural innovation finds new ways of connecting existing components.

Radical innovation connects new components (or concepts) in new ways. The components and concepts may only be marginally different yet the combination overcomes some previous limitation. This can extend possibilities beyond present constraints in surprisingly powerful ways.

How to use?

Look at what you are attempting to improve. Maybe you are trying to improve on what your competitors are doing. Perhaps you are trying to improve on your own work. Or the way that something is done generally or traditionally. Consider the individual parts and their connections.

Think about each component. There is generally an obvious path to improvement. Or at least an obvious kind of improvement to make something faster, bigger, smaller or more dependable. The improvement tends to follow a path of previous improvement. Then consider new components with a new approach that could replace existing components.

Think about connections. If you reorganise the way existing components are put together, you may be able to make improvements. You may find ways of exceeding existing limitations that do not really involve new technological boundaries.

Finally think about how components and connections may both be changed. If you make isolated changes they may fail to produce the desired improvements. Alternatively, if you make imaginative changes to one, then those changes can create opportunities to change the other in radical ways.

Key questions

- How does the thing you want to improve work? What does the thing you want to improve achieve for the person using it? What are the costs of using the thing? What are the main components of the thing to be improved? How do those components link to each other?
- Are there any bottle-necks in the existing system? Are there components that produce more than the overall system can use? Is there any characteristic of the overall system that could be improved by changing the way components link together?
- Can you think of examples where radical success has come from incremental improvements? How can you work with other groups to change the design of components or connections? Who has to be convinced to work with you to allow big picture innovation?

Related ideas

The **theory of constraints** proposed by Eliyahu M. Goldratt and Jeff Cox, suggests that there is always at least one constraint in any system. If that constraint is in the components then you would want to improve the component. If the constraint is in the connections (or linkages) then the connections need to be improved. You can go further and improve the overall system in the direction that gives the greatest benefit to people using it.

case study

Innovation in action

People like clean clothes but hate washing them. This desire has led to progressively better washing machines. From the first patented hand-driven machine in 1691, millions of electric washing machines in the 1920s and the first automatic washing machine in 1937. In the 1990s, washing machines gained microcontrollers and the ability to weigh the load and automatically select the wash cycle. But it was not until the 21st century that a team of innovators in Leeds, England, finally created the Xeros waterless washing machine and LG, in Korea, created the Steam Closet. You hang your clothes in what looks like a fridge and wait for it to remove unwanted smells and wrinkles.

Rogers' adoption and diffusion curve

For your new idea to make a difference it needs to find its way to people who will find it useful. The idea is passed around from person to person until it reaches someone who can put it to work. If your best ideas don't reach the people who will use them, nothing will happen as a result. It will be as if the new ideas had never existed. Many ideas follow (more or less) an s-shaped path including adoption, hype, and performance.

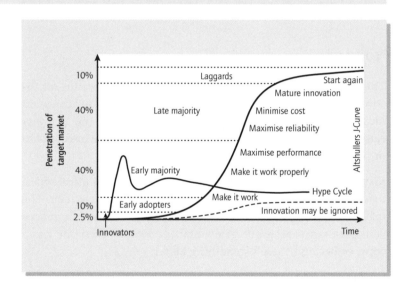

Innovator's insights

People share ideas in various ways. Ideas can be shared by talking about them, or writing about them, or using those ideas and then being seen by others doing so. The idea may be contained inside a skill, a habit or a language, service, object or product.

People adopt innovations after learning about the new ideas, being persuaded to have an opinion (good or bad), deciding whether to try it out, implementing the idea and finally adopting, rejecting or re-inventing the innovation. Choices are based on relative advantage, compatibility, complexity, testability and observ- ability. Such decisions may be individual, collective or enforced.

Any existing idea is somewhere on the adoption curve, the performance curve or hype curve. You can find out the minimum potential value (or popularity) of your new idea by looking at the popularity (or market) for existing ideas. It can help you look for idea friction (why various groups haven't adopted the idea) and then figure out how to smooth the adoption of your new idea. You can build new ideas that help existing ideas by overcoming their limitations. You can also create ideas that play with or against existing ideas.

How to use?

Think about your organisation and where what it does fits on the adoption curve. Maybe you need people to help you turn your idea into something that works. Or your idea exists but at a very early (unfinished) stage so you need innovators, newness addicts or people who appreciate the value.

Maybe your idea is already past the mainstream and must appeal to laggards, those who drag their feet about any new idea. You may need to simplify how it is used, explained or sold. Or maybe your idea is running out of popularity, because everyone has a copy, or because there's something better.

Consider whether (and how) your idea is facing competition. Those ideas could be old ideas (products, concepts, services) that are traditional or just dominant. Or those ideas could be new ideas (products, concepts, services) that are challenging the dominant position of your old idea. Or there could be a swarm of new ideas that are all trying to become successful and popular.

It's easy to assume that ideas all slavishly follow the curve, or the s-shape. The people you work with may look at similar ideas in the past and think that they have to pursue a similar path of popularity. Yet ideas can be swept away at any stage.

One second, at the peak of the hype cycle, they are the hot, new, new thing among innovation-lovers. The next moment they are replaced, due to changes in fashion or technological obsolescence. Other ideas never become widely popular (shown by the dashed curve at the bottom of the chart). Or new ideas can bypass the typical trend-setters and jump to the majority. The disruptive big bang.

Don't be trapped by lazy assumptions about how people adopt new ideas. The diffusion curve is just a model that describes one way they are adopted – not the complete picture. It's also important that you are not blindsided by what you want to be true. People often assume they have time to respond and adapt to new ideas because the adoption s-curves have the power to predict the future. They don't.

Key questions

- Do enough people know about your idea? How easy is your idea to understand? What is the relative advantage of your new idea over existing ideas? What weaknesses does your new idea have over other new ideas? Is the challenge the idea or the way you're explaining it?

- Does your new idea fit with the way that people work or live? Is your idea compatible with other ideas, products or services? Can it be made compatible? Can you build the other things that people will need before your idea works? Can you get others to build them?

- Is your idea easy to use? Is your idea too difficult to use? Can your idea be made more usable so that the value is greater than the pain of using it? (see Making new ideas useful on page 74). Is it easy for people to try out your new idea? Have you got samples available? Or free trials? Or reviews online?

- Where can people watch your idea being used? Who can you get to use your idea, product or service? Who influences opinion? When do people get to share experiences with your kind of idea, product or service? (see Making innovation popular on page 105).

Related ideas

Disruptive innovation, popularised by Clayton Christensen suggests existing ideas can be predictably disrupted by new ideas in the form of products that are cheaper and look after neglected groups. With low-end success, the new ideas can gain the resources (and popularity) necessary to appeal to more and more groups until they topple the existing leaders.

Big-bang disruption, described by Larry Downes and Paul F. Nunes, is one alternative that recognises how innovators can skip the low-to-high route and disrupt from anywhere at any time with complete, better-in-every-way innovations.

---

case study

Innovation in action

When a new way of doing something replaces the old way, this is disruption. People don't use printed road maps anymore – sales declined 50% over the past five years – because GPS navigation in the car – or on your phone – is faster and easier. It seems incredibly big-bang until you remember that the satellites that provide GPS signals were first conceived of in 1973 and not operational until 1995. Most radical innovation is shockingly slow, then shockingly fast. Surf well.

Abernathy and Utterback's three phases of innovation

Innovations are hybrid ideas. They are made of old ideas. They are made of new ideas. They are made of ideas related to products, or things. They are made of ideas supported by processes, or ways of doing things. Successful innovation tends to lead to a particular winning combination of products and processes. This dominant design wins until beaten by something new.

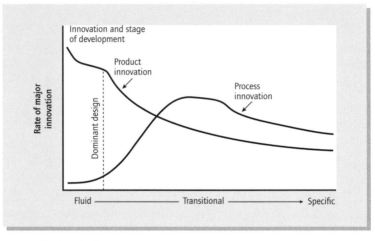

Innovator's insights

As an innovator, you will be faced with many different forces. You've got innovation in product, innovation in processes, actions of competitors (and competing ideas) and the actions of people inside your own organisation. These forces tend to follow certain semi-predictable patterns.

The fluid phase is about many people trying many different ways of making a big new idea work. No-one knows which design will be the best. No-one knows which design will be the most popular. In the very earliest phase, there may be enthusiasts trying to figure out the mechanics of the new idea. Sometimes this involves friendly collaboration. Sometimes there is intense rivalry. But because no-one knows what will work, the competition is between designs rather than for huge markets.

The transitional phase involves some kind of (gradual) standardisation. People are starting to like the innovation. Innovators have figured out how to make the idea work at some level. Designs tend to converge on fewer competing designs. Eventually one general (dominant) design becomes accepted. Every version of the innovation tends to have common elements. But people try and find new ways of making their version of the innovation different. Or make it seem different.

The specific phase moves to other parts of the innovation for particular customers. You might compete on costs or features – but also on the services that surround the innovation. The brainpower tends to be focused on keeping interest alive in the original innovation. But many are unwilling to make the time and money gambles on moving beyond the dominant design.

How to use?

Try and identify different phases for different products or ideas. If you're in a fluid phase, you can try to establish the winning (dominant) design. Some of this is about what is best. Some of winning is about being first. Some is about attracting interest. Or winning by making friends in influential places. There are events inside and outside your control. You can hang back and spot the winner or learn from losing designs. You can learn enough to benefit regardless of which design wins.

If there is already a dominant design, you have decisions to make. Innovation can be inside the dominant design, outside the dominant design, supportive of the dominant design or built to disrupt the dominant design. Some people win by protecting the design. Others win by specialising around the dominant design. Victory through efficient focus versus success through radically new ideas (see performance curve, or J-curve on page 216).

Key questions

- Do you want to reach beyond the limits of the dominant design? Can you provide more for less to people who don't want more? Or provide different for those who want different? How can you make the dominant design last longer by adding services?

- Are you in a fluid, transitional or specific phase? Do you understand the dangers and possibilities of new ideas that are still in a fluid phase? Do you want to support existing designs? Do you want to win by disrupting the dominant design? What features are demanded by the dominant design?

Related ideas

Old innovation can stop new innovation. People try to protect the success of existing ideas. They may find it easier to contribute to making the best of the existing innovation. Sometimes, this means that creativity may restrict itself to improvement *within* the limits of the existing approach. So creative people can waste time on reconfiguring rather than revolutionising. This is a risk in any closed system – like engineers working on the Trabant in East Germany unable to build new manufacturing facilities, or scientists working on genetics in the USA who were not legally permitted to use embryonic stem cells.

---

case study

Innovation in action

In the late 1970s, France was one of the first countries to have a nationwide information network with a console in every home. The Minitel, a kind of small desktop computer, could access online shopping, chat and information more than a decade before the rest of the world, but, because it was so good, slowed French involvement in the Worldwide Web. First and best can get in the way of second and better.

Chesbrough's open innovation

No innovation is an island. Nor can innovators be successful if isolated. Yet it is tempting to hide innovation efforts from the world, to avoid our best ideas being copied. If you do all the work yourself, you may be able to keep your idea secret. But doing all the work yourself is usually more expensive than being open to the ideas of others. Closed innovation can be so slow it fails.

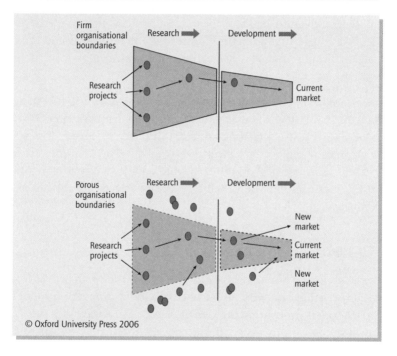

© Oxford University Press 2006

Innovator's insights

Closed innovation is a particular approach to making new ideas work. It became traditional in very large corporations that invested heavily in their own research and development (R&D). Big R&D departments moved all the way from ideas to real-world innovation. The idea was to hold on to the benefits of innovation by owning the process from beginning to end. The system was closed.

Open innovation is an alternative approach to making new ideas work. It argues that closed systems cannot be as effective in experimentation as open systems. You can spend all that money on ideas that a closed group produce and then find that someone else has produced something much better. Or you can reject the very best ideas because they weren't invented or developed in your own labs.

If you follow the closed innovation model too slavishly, you may suffer from innovation dead-ends or just be too slow at getting somewhere good. You may do great work but not be rewarded. Closed innovation has to choose too few ideas far too soon. So it makes sense that someone, somewhere may make something succeed simply because there are so many innovators out there working hard.

If you follow open innovation too blindly, you may stop investing in your own new ideas. Leaders may stop trusting their own people to create solutions or revolutionise processes. There's a significant danger of losing creative skills and attitudes. You become a consumer of other people's ideas without contributing anything new or valuable. Outsourcing creativity can be a mistake.

How to use?

Look at how your organisation works with new ideas. Think about whether you work more like the closed innovation model or the open innovation model. If new ideas always (or nearly always) come from inside the group then you may be missing out. If you always develop new ideas inside the group rather than buying or borrowing off-the-shelf new ideas, you may also be missing out.

The open innovation model thinks that external brain power is just as important as internal brain power. The open innovation model considers ideas surrounding *how* to use the innovation as just as important as the innovation itself. The way of making the innovation successful (the business model) matters. The best approach to using a new idea needs more than a lone, scientific genius.

Closed innovation tends to pick winners and losers very early in the game. That's natural. It would be difficult to do anything else. New ideas take time to develop; time is limited so you have to choose. The problem is that your choice may lead to an innovation that isn't successful. Your early choices may also reject successful innovations that seemed risky or bizarre or unattractive.

Open innovation lets in the world. If an outside idea is better – or is simply a better fit – then it is welcome to make a contribution. If you discover that mass experimentation (and luck) outside has created something that you can really use, it makes sense to embrace that idea. You actively connect your people (and business) with external news from universities, inventors, users and entrepreneurs.

Key questions

- Do you give equal importance to internal and external knowledge and ideas? How can you improve discussions about the fit between innovation and business models? When will you be spending time exploring different ways of getting the value out of the new idea?

- What new ideas have you rejected? How can you spread your innovation bets? Are you willing (and able) to cut your losses on internal ideas if external ideas are better? How can you increase the external/internal flow of ideas?

- How can you share what you discover – or invent – with the outside world? Can you sell your new ideas without developing them? Do you proactively – and imaginatively – manage your intellectual property? Do you work with innovation intermediaries? How do you measure your innovation capability and performance?

Related ideas

There are many different ways of opening up the innovation process. Consider these three examples: The Vienna Tourist Board asked 650,000 people to contribute 'new, unconventional and provocative proposals' for making the city the most attractive destination in Europe. No Right Brain Left Behind is a campaign for increasing creativity education that connects professionals in the creative industries with schools to solve problems together. Innocentive is an open-innovation match-maker that emerged from efforts by Eli Lilly, the pharmaceutical giant, to increase innovation and collaboration through the internet. You can pick and mix your own unique solution.

---

case study

Innovation in action

The word *shanzhai* once described production and sales of imitation products in China often derided as lacking creativity. Yet research from Jiangning Zhao, Catholic University of Korea, suggests *shanzhai* is a powerful, open-innovation model for catching up with competitors. Copying products is an effective way of transferring skills and building clusters of related partners.

Innovation comes because *shanzhai* involves copying with a twist. Firms lower costs to compete with bigger brands, simplify products to maximise the priorities of local customers (good-enough) and move faster than market leaders. Firms start by copy-catting and grey-market counterfeiting but move to originality and open hubs with a methodology of interchangeable components that outperforms the corporations they once copied. Many *shanzhai* innovators are now global brands.

March's exploration vs. exploitation

Successful adaptation is often about balancing exploration and exploitation. If you spend all your time using what you know, you are less likely to learn what you don't know. Yet if you spend all your time exploring what you don't know, you are less likely to grab the opportunities you find.

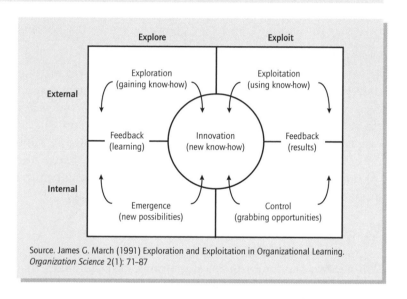

Source. James G. March (1991) Exploration and Exploitation in Organizational Learning. *Organization Science* 2(1): 71–87

Innovator's insights

Exploration is about finding out what you don't know. Exploring is a deliberate attempt to gain new know-how. And only by exploring can you find new opportunities to exploit. The process of exploration involves you playing with new ideas (or old ideas in new situations).

Exploitation is more about using the know-how you already have. You learn about whether what you know is working when a real-world environment gives you success (or failure). This feedback may change the way you refine the way you do things. You may choose differently next time but your choices are mainly focused on increasing efficiency and getting what you know done right.

All exploitation makes competition about who can do the same thing best. You get locked in to one way of doing things. And you may even lose the ability to adapt flexibly because the focus becomes one of perfection rather than innovation.

If you focus only on exploration, you'll pay the costs of experimenting but rarely get the benefits of improved results. You may learn many things about many things but not develop the skills necessary to use that knowledge. Your group may also become future fixated rather than getting things done.

At extremes of success or failure, people tend to stick to what they know. You need to remember the benefits of exploration even when exploitation is giving such great results. People learn the organisational code from what other people do and what is explicitly taught. These lead to individual beliefs. At the same time, individual beliefs lead to actions that can change the organisational code. Both groups can get things wrong because no-one is certain to be right – especially about the future.

How to use?

You need to explore to increase the range of possibilities that you can then choose between. Exploring increases variation while also allowing experimentation to see what works and what doesn't. Just as important it allows you to learn flexibility that is a form of new (improved) know-how.

Any work on exploration is a risk. It's automatically uncertain. Whereas in the short term, exploitation of what has worked in the past is likely to work in the future. The problem is that the future is changing, and becoming world class at what the world no longer wants is failure.

Look at how much time you spend on exploration of new ideas versus exploitation. This will typically vary by individual, team and hierarchical level. Think about the levels of change in your situation, market or environment. Consider the likely sources of future disruption or crisis.

Ideally you want the organisation to deal with a lot of learning in a flexible, abstract way. You don't want people to think that what they think they know is reality. You want to avoid people turning the way you're currently doing things into traditions or habits too quickly. And certainly not rigidly.

You need thinking that deviates from the way things are done *at the moment*. Without that kind of deviance, there is no progress because there can be no learning. So you need differences in people to ensure that the organisation doesn't become stuck. It's powerful when everyone understands this.

Key questions

- How much time is spent exploring versus exploiting? Is your learning process too fixed, too fast and too final? Who is challenging the organisational code? Is there enough difference in opinions and experience? Is your training too effective to allow innovation? (see innovators' clubs on page 245).

- Do you have the ability to learn fast and then unlearn fast? Who is spending time playing and experimenting? How can you ensure that there is enough slack resource to encourage experimentation?

- What hierarchical level is closest to the reality that matters to success? Is your boardroom or your front line closest to the customers that matter? Are your technicians or your senior management team most intimate with the technologies and trends that shape the future?

- How far does diversity in your organisation reflect your need for future innovation? Is your innovation focused on operational improvement or strategic disruption? Is your people turnover too high for new know-how to be used? Or is your turnover too low for new ideas?

Related ideas

To cope with the demands of exploring new ideas and exploiting existing ideas, sometimes a separate group is responsible for exploration. Overall such a group often helps – and it tends to help manufacturing more than service firms. Not surprisingly, organisations focused on exploring new ideas are often valued more highly, but, in cash flow, perform a little worse. They gain a reputation for inventing the future rather than maximising the here and now. It may appear obvious that becoming the best at exploring *and* exploiting is wise, but a choice is usually wiser in the long term.

---

case study

Innovation in action

Half-Life is a game published by Valve Corporation. It has about 400 employees and a very unusual culture. Its aim is to have a flat structure where there is no management and everyone has a say over who is hired, fired and how much they are paid. This has allowed the company to explore new opportunities in games, online retail and living-room technology. Although it also creates problems when the traditions of the hidden power structure get in the way of bringing in people with different opinions. The truth is, as Bob Sutton, professor of Management Science at Stanford, argues, that hierarchy is inevitable but that doesn't mean that all hierarchies are equally effective or ineffective. Hierarchies depend on culture shaped by choices.

Johnson and Johnson's constructive controversy cycle

No idea is ever perfect. And when people pretend that an idea is perfect or finished, others are less likely to try and improve it. This leaves the idea untested and stagnant. It also prevents engagement with the idea that will develop the innovation thinking of everyone working with the idea. It is far more powerful to create constructive controversy as a way of engaging and opening minds.

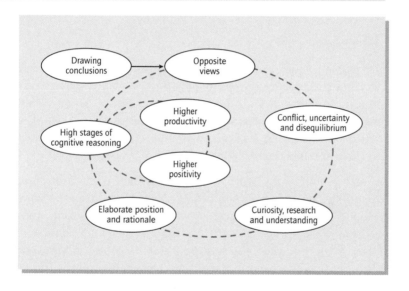

Innovator's insights

Lack of controversy can prevent an idea being tested rigorously. Avoiding conflict can stop people becoming intellectually and emotionally engaged with an idea or subject. If you don't engage with an idea then you may have less understanding of how the idea actually works (or doesn't work). You are also less likely to spend time improving the idea or find something better.

Constructive controversy is a technique that deliberately sets out to create conflict. When new ideas are dismissed too easily, there is no controversy because everyone has agreed that the idea is not to be pursued. When new ideas are accepted too easily, there is no conflict because no-one has taken the time to consider alternatives. Ideas may be treated as facts when they are not.

You can use constructive controversy to test, and expand, specific ideas. You can also use constructive controversy to develop your ability to think better. The ability of individuals and groups to be logically rigorous *and* radically creative can be increased. This is a divergent thinking skill that becomes part of the way things are done which leads to doing things (very) differently.

How to use

Step 1 is all about getting people to do their homework – and draw conclusions from their investigation. *Step 2* involves people finding opposing views from their conclusions – actual differences in the views of those involved, different views that exist outside of the group and also new differences that are created logically and imaginatively by the group.

In *Step 3* your group will experience conflict, uncertainty and disequilibrium as they face opposing views drawn from the same evidence. You don't want so much conflict that the group stops cooperating but you do want enough conflict for imaginative focus. As an innovator, you want to influence others to love your ideas but you also need to have those ideas tested by the minds of others. You should be open to better versions of your original idea and also to ideas that are more valuable and more beautiful than your original idea. Everyone should be more driven in *Step 4* to seek a better understanding so that they can either improve or reject their existing ideas.

Curiosity leads to research. Research leads to understanding. In *Step 5* ideas can be elaborated along with the rationale for believing in them. Holes that are picked in the original ideas allow light to reach the unexplored and under-examined. In *Step*

6 the power of opposing views can inspire innovators to reach higher levels of reasoning with accompanying higher productivity *and* improved self-image. You feel better because your idea is more complete, more robust and more beautiful.

Key questions

- Is your idea complete? Do you know where your idea is weak? What are the opposing views to your own opinion? Has enough time been invested in competing ideas? What are the most convincing alternatives to your idea? Do you have the facts to back up your opinion?

- Who can challenge your idea? Do you have a process for challenging ideas? Does your role or reputation stop rigorous discussion? What parts of your idea are underdeveloped? How can you get motivated enough to detail the arguments, rationale and mechanisms of your idea? Does your idea need stress-testing?

- Is it better to experience pain early or late in the process? Do you have a way of learning fast *before* implementing? How can you learn fast (over and over again) before it's too late? Do you have too much consensus? Is there excessive agreement? How can you harness conflict?

- Have you identified logical fallacies in your ideas? Have you spotted the blind spots? Can you hire people to spot the blind spots for you? What is it about your idea that is blindingly right inside the organisation and blindingly wrong outside the organisation?

Related ideas

Successful innovators are better at integrating constructive conflict, according to research from Michael Song of Henry Bloch School of Business, and Barbara Dyer of MIT. Organisations that fail with innovation tend to force people into agreeing – or hiding disagreement. People in failing firms avoid discussing differences, which stops them learning from diverse perspectives or resolving destructive conflict. This unresolved conflict damages relationships and prevents understanding. Generally it's better to openly use complaints and opinions as ingredients for innovation.

Innovation in action

Curious Honda engineers kept working on dreams for a new kind of private jet even after the project had officially been cancelled. They kept working for 10 years before presenting their revolutionary designs to the senior managers as part of *waigaya*, a word that describes the sound of passionate disagreement. In 2014, the innovative Honda Jet went into production with above-the-wing engine pods and 30% more cabin space. Honda believes in the power of dreams *and* conflict.

Powell and Grodal's networks for innovation

There are rigid and fluid networks. There are formal and informal networks. Some networks are based on contractual relationships. Other networks are based on common obsessions. High-trust or low-trust networks. Not all networks are equal. And not all networks are equal for innovation.

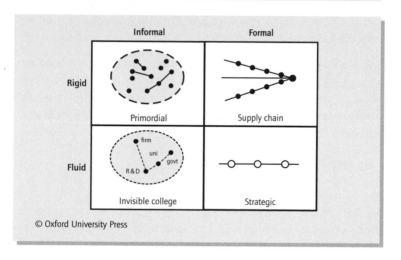

© Oxford University Press

Innovator's insights

Difference is necessary to novelty. And novelty is essential to innovation. Networks bring different people and different people bring new ideas. Things that seem obvious in one area or market can be huge insights in another area or market. Facts or skills that are necessary to making an innovation work are often only available outside of your organisation or team. Innovators need networks.

Primordial networks have similar people connected who share a common social identity. They work together within a community that exists before the specific innovation. The new ideas are something that the group works on together because members share similar values, problems, needs and interests.

Invisible colleges involve people who are similar *and* different. They are a great way of discovering new ideas very quickly. There are highly fluid ties between groups including firms, universities, governments and R&D groups. The connections are informal. They are often also temporary.

Supply chains exist to produce something specific. The connections tend to be between groups who can provide different parts of the production process. There is a common work identity between group members. Membership of the group is closed and based on contractual relationships.

Strategic networks also have different kinds of people and organisations. Membership of such networks is very fluid – even though there is a contractual basis for working together. The reasons for working together tend to emerge through deliberate attempts to create relationships.

How to use?

Look at your innovation needs and objectives. All four kinds of innovation network are useful in different ways. You benefit from building trust and understanding in your network. This takes time that must be invested for the long term. Strong ties and effective day-to-day working relationships can be easier if members of your network are local. Or the group finds virtual working natural.

You are more likely to get different kinds of new idea from people that you don't know well. These weak ties with dissimilar people are a very effective way of provoking new insights. Strangers can easily see your problems differently or give you information that you would never have found. These new insights can be taken back to closed working networks where strong relationships make it easier to develop ideas into practical innovations.

The strength of one kind of network is the weakness of another. Building strong relationships is excellent for the day-to-day process of development but gradually reduces the creativity range of new ideas. People learn to be similar but innovation needs difference. The life cycle of networks means that you need to keep creating and developing new generations of connections.

Key questions

■ What kinds of innovation networks do you work with? Are your innovation efforts mainly focused internally? What kind of time is invested in informal networks? Which primordial networks are most important as a source of craft-based skills and insight?

■ How does your invisible college work? How effective is your invisible college? What are your learning connections with government, universities and other firms? Do you follow the work of particular academics? Who is responsible for keeping new ideas flowing?

■ Which parts of your network are strategic? Are there relationships you need to protect or formalise? How do you keep developing new generations of strategic and supply-chain networks? Do you need more new connections or deeper working relationships?

■ How do you generate your own new knowledge? Are you combining and developing your new knowledge with people in your networks? What do you contribute to your networks? To what extent are you central or prominent in your networks? What is your reputation?

Related ideas

Innovation may be everywhere but it's not equally distributed. To get the right team around your new idea, it's smart to look around for clusters of expertise that can help. Johnson & Johnson have set up one-stop-shops in four innovation hot spots – China, London, Boston and California – with teams who have the authority and expertise to make deals with local entrepreneurs and scientists. You could do something similar by making connections with people in the innovation hot spots that matter to your innovation aspirations. It's not a big budget strategy, it's a big brain strategy.

---

case study

Innovation in action

Recently a Dutch designer – Dave Hakkens – had the idea for an upgradable modular phone. He called his new idea 'Phonebloks' and created a primordial network of a million enthusiasts around his idea. Meanwhile, Motorola reached out to Hakkens as part of its invisible college network. Next, there will be a strategic network of developers for modules rather like smartphone apps in an app store. Each module will be able to fit into a basic phone structure that they call an endoskeleton. Key components, including the endoskeleton, will be manufactured by a supply-chain network. If successful, the modular phone idea will depend on all four kinds of innovation networks.

Boyd's OODA loop

Innovations are in competition with other innovations. Innovators are competing with innovators. The innovator that adapts fastest to the situation – or adapts the situation fastest – is likely to be successful. You can improve your handling of complex situations by using insights from the OODA loop. You move from observing what is happening through to acting on what you have observed.

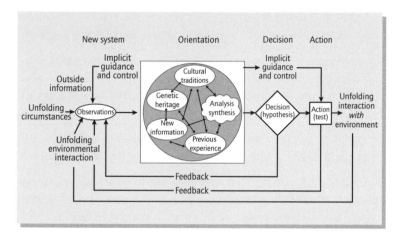

Innovator's insights

Your innovation will have to be fitted into its circumstance. Since the circumstance will continue to change, that means that you will have to change. Understanding a fast-moving situation faster than the competition – or faster than your cash reserves running out – is valuable. You can use innovation to adapt faster. You can adapt your innovation to fit what is happening in the world. And you can adapt your approach so that you can complete cycles of innovation faster and faster.

Any innovation is part of (at least) two complex systems. There is the system that the innovation attempts to change (or improve). There is also the system that produces, develops and adopts the innovation. These complex systems have many parts, many feedback loops and have hidden behaviours. No single person or model can ever describe the full behaviour of any complex system.

Complex systems cannot be completely understood because they can't be fully seen. With innovation, you're adding more unknowns to an already unknowable situation. The people who can respond most rapidly *and* intelligently are more likely to adapt successfully.

Observing is about being able to see what is happening. If you can't see the action then you can't respond to real-world events. Innovators thrive on information, feedback and getting involved.

Orienting combines what you already know with what you've just discovered. The way you process knowledge is affected by your nature, nurture and culture. You analyse, synthesise and reorient.

Deciding takes your new position and examines alternatives. As an innovator, you hypothesise about the causes of events and the next possible steps. The danger is getting stuck in a thinking rut.

Acting is what you do. You may respond to new information or ignore it. You could consider too much and never get around to action. Fast or slow decisions can lead to success or failure.

The loop creates feedback. You act according to your understanding. Your actions lead to outcomes. These outcomes give new information about whether your understanding is helpful. Maybe you were wrong and can change your mind. Maybe you were right and need to keep going.

How to use?

Innovation is about the unknown. You can only guess what will happen when you throw a new idea into a real-world situation. You're unlikely to succeed the first time you try to make a new idea work. The important thing is to pay attention to what happens as a result of what you try to do. You win valuable feedback about what to try next. You can deliberately experiment to learn more.

The original purpose of the OODA loop was to move faster through each cycle than an opponent. Some people focus on their own speed while others focus on slowing down the opposition. If you get ahead, you have room to make smarter decisions for the next loop. Meanwhile the competition has less space and is under more pressure. They are likely to make bad (or no) decisions.

Smart innovators can cycle from observation to action faster than their competitors. You start with what you *can* do and innovate your way to something better. You operate in rapid loops that test new ideas against reality. There is the external environment where your idea will be used *and* the internal culture that will shape whether – or how – your new idea will be used.

Key questions

- Are you good at observation? How can you gather information better? What is your process for keeping up to date with new events? How quickly do you learn from rapid experiments? When something goes wrong, are you guided by cultural traditions or by new information?

- Can you create short cycles rather than big projects? Would your people benefit from training in analysis and synthesis? How can you get out of bad habits that block learning? How can you design tests of new (and old) ideas into your work?

- Do you hang out with the people who have the problems you're trying to solve? Do you know the people who understand the solutions you're going to need?

Related ideas

For innovation, be as close as possible to change. According to work by Fiona Schweitzer and Oliver Gassmann, innovation is only exceptional if there is 'an active search for latent needs, weak signals and emerging trends' rather than 'just following the evident and palpable'. That's why Cisco ran an ideas competition and then invested $10 million in the winning idea submitted by an IT student. It's yet another way of going outside the obvious to find non-obvious insights that can shape the future.

case study

Innovation in action

Yahoo! Japan is a joint venture with Softbank from Japan. Often worth more than its parent company, it has always been profitable and reaches over 80% of Japanese internet users. Since the start, it has out-innovated its rivals (including Google and eBay). Fast observation allowed it to see opportunities. Through fast orientation, it has adapted to local needs better than the competition.

The company has used local knowledge to orient itself better to Japanese tastes. It understood the value of sponsorship – like the Yahoo! Fukuoka Dome. It made decisions faster than non-Japanese companies because it was free of a US corporate process. It created Yahoo! TV with Sharp and provide broadband services. It acted faster then and still keep adapting to what it learns.

Final words

'The reasonable man adapts himself to the world; the unreasonable one persists in trying to adapt the world to himself. Therefore all progress depends on the unreasonable man.'
George Bernard Shaw

The principles in this book are based on the advice of the greatest innovators all the way to the 21st century. They are also based on enduring evidence and cutting-edge wisdom from the world's leading scientists. Some of their work is directly about innovation; some findings are from the psychology of creativity, other useful ideas from the sociology of revolution and evolutionary economics. Everything has been selected with loving care.

Each model in the innovator's toolkit is worth understanding and putting into practice. There is more to know about each one. Some of this knowledge will come from other books but mainly by the effort of playing with the ideas in real-life situations. This will be a valuable investment of your time which will reward you and develop your ability to turn new ideas into success.

This isn't a book you should scan, put down and forget about. It's a book about living innovation where ideas are not forgotten but move from drawing board to improving the status quo. It's important that you use it well. Jot notes in the margins, read it in the bath, shove it into your bag. Write your own new ideas down. Underline what matters to you.

It doesn't matter if it gets wrecked. It matters that you can use it and gain the working knowledge to become a powerful innovator who can create new ideas and then make those beautiful ideas useful to other people. You will be able to find friends for each brainchild and surf the chaotic waves until something worthwhile has been achieved.

You will use new ideas strategically to shape your future when old ideas are not enough. You will start to see the shape of innovation, guess the next steps, anticipate the next problem and shape events intelligently. You will learn how to use innovation to improve your own life and our world.

Innovation + Strategy = Adaptability

The Innovation Book is part of a trilogy that includes *The Strategy Book* and *Adaptability*. So it's worth explaining a little more about how they fit together.

Innovation is about creating new ideas and making those new ideas useful. It's a form of practical creativity that extends human ability beyond what was previously possible.

Strategy is about shaping the future. It's about finding the smartest, shortest way to desirable ends with available means. It is our ability to act on imagined alternatives.

Adaptability is about recognising the need to adapt. It's about understanding the necessary adaptation and then adapting as needed. All success is successful adaptation. You can adapt to your situation or adapt your situation, adapt ourselves to our environment or adapt your situation to your desires and dreams.

The books share principles but only a few models and examples. You can bring the ideas in the three books together by making notes that connect strategy to innovation and adaptability. In your innovators' clubs, move from one to the other. Think like a strategist, create like an innovator, and transcend limitations through a high-adaptability, high-achievement focus.

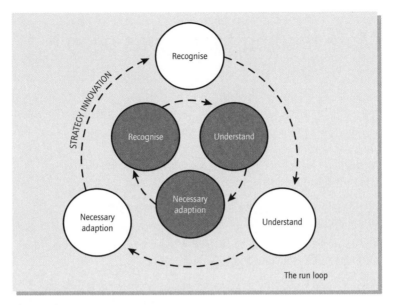

The run loop

The run loop

Do this now!

Start an innovators' club to encourage and develop creativity, learning, and bold collective action.

You can use *The Innovation Book* as a quick, dirty, and scalable approach to increasing innovation. Get people together for an hour a week for six weeks. It's a simple commitment. Each week discuss each part of the book. Vary the location. Use webcams. Experiment with Twitter chats. Have breakfast. Go for a walk. Meet in a playground. Try out the ideas. And inspire each other. Introduce *The Strategy Book*. Encourage other innovator's clubs throughout your network or firm. Expand.

And then let me know how you're changing the world on Twitter: @maxmckeown

'Optimism, pessimism, f**k that; we're going to make it happen...'
Elon Musk, Space X

More reading for curious people

Altshuller, G., *40 Principles: TRIZ Keys to Technical Innovation* (Technical Innovation Center, 2002).

Altshuller, G., *And Suddenly the Inventor Appeared* (Technical Innovation Center, 2004).

Anthony, S. D., *The Little Black Book of Innovation: How it Works, How to Do It* (Harvard Business Review Press, 2012).

Boyd, D. and Goldenberg, J., *Inside the Box: Why the Best Business Innovations are Right in Front of You* (Profile Books, 2013).

Burgelman, R. A., Christensen, C. M. and Wheelright, S. C., *Strategic Management of Technology and Innovation,* fifth edition (McGraw-Hill, 2008).

Christensen, C. M., *The Innovator's Dilemma* (Harvard Business Review, 1997).

Christensen, C. M. and Raynor, M. E., *The Innovator's Solution: Creating and Sustaining Successful Growth* (Harvard Business School Press, 2003).

Diamond, J., *Guns, Germs and Steel: A Short History of Everybody for the Last 13,000 Years* (Vintage, 1998).

Dodgson, M., Gann, D. M. and Phillips, N., *The Oxford Handbook of Innovation Management* (Oxford University Press, 2013).

Duggan, W., *Strategic Intuition* (Columbia Business School, 2007).

Dyer, J., Gregersen, H. and Christensen, C. M., *The Innovator's DNA* (Harvard Business School, 2011).

Fagerberg, J., Mowery, D. C. and Nelson, R. R., *Oxford Handbook of Innovation* (Oxford University Press, 2005).

HBR's 10 Must Reads on Innovation (Harvard Business Review, 2013).

Jetten, J. and Hornsey, M. J., *Rebels in Groups: Dissent, Deviance, Difference and Defiance* (Wiley-Blackwell, 2011).

Keeley, L., Pikkel, R., Quinn, B. and Walters, H., *Ten Types of Innovation: The Discipline of Breakthroughs* (Wiley, 2013).

Kingdon, M., *The Science of Serendipity: How to Unlock the Promise of Innovation in Large Organizations* (Wiley, 2012).

Kirton, M. J., *Adaption-innovation: In the Context of Diversity and Change* (Routledge, 2003).

Leavitt, H. J., Pondy, L. R. and Boje, D. M., *Readings in Managerial Psychology,* fourth edition (The University of Chicago Press, 1989).

Leonard, D. and Swap, W., *Deep Smarts: How to Cultivate and Transfer Enduring Business Wisdom* (Harvard Business School Press, 2005).

Maital, S. and Shesadri, D. V. R., *Innovation Management: Strategies, Concepts and Tools for Growth and Profit,* second edition (SAGE India, 2012).

Malerba, F. and Brusoni, S., *Perspectives on Innovation* (Cambridge, 2007).

Mckeown, M. *Adaptability* (Kogan Page, 2012).

Mckeown, M. *The Strategy Book* (Pearson, 2012).

Mckeown, M. *The Truth about Innovation* (Pearson, 2008).

Miller, P. and Wedell-Wedellsborg, T., *Innovation As Usual: How to Help Your People Bring Great Ideas to Life* (Harvard Business Review Press, 2013).

Moore, G. A., *Crossing The Chasm* (Harper Business Essentials, 1991).

Phelps, E., *Mass Flourishing: How Grassroots Innovation Created Jobs, Challenges and Change* (Princeton, 2013).

Poole, M. S. and Van de Ven, A. H., *Handbook of Organizational Change and Innovation* (Oxford University Press, 2004).

Ries, E., *The Lean Startup: How Constant Innovation Creates Radically Successful Businesses* (Penguin, 2011).

Rogers, E. M., *Diffusion of Innovation*, fifth edition (Free Press, Simon & Schuster, 2003).

Rosenhead, J., *Rational Analysis for a Problematic World Revisited:*

Problem Structuring Methods for Complexity, Uncertainty and Conflict, second edition (John Wiley, 2001).

Sternberg, R. J. *Handbook of Creativity* (Cambridge University Press, 1999).

Tidd, J. and Bessant, J., *Managing Innovation: Integrating Technological, Market and Organizational Change,* fifth edition (John Wiley, 2013).

Tushman, M. and Anderson, P. C. *Managing Strategic Innovation and Change,* second edition (Oxford University Press, 2004).

Van de Ven, A., Polley, D. E., Garud, R., Venkataraman, S., *The Innovation Journey* (Oxford University Press, 2008).

Wulfen, G. van, *The Innovation Expedition* (BIS Publishers, 2013).

Index

minimum winning game (MWG)
93, 154–6
Minitel 222
minorities 118
mistakes 108, 138, 159
monitoring 89
Moore, Geoffrey 184
Moore's law 103
Moscovici, Serge 118
Moser, Alfredo 111
motivation 58–63, 80, 114, 117, 124,
168–70
demotivation 169
extrinsic 168–9
intrinsic 168–9
Motorola 238
Moutai, Kweichow 51
Mozilla 141
Mulally, Alan 123
Musk, Elon 244

names 110
NASA 58
Netflix 97, 103
networks 14, 37, 111, 235, 238 see
also communities and groups
building 36
closed 46
fluid 46, 55, 235
formal 46, 235
high-trust 235
informal 46, 235, 237
invisible college 235–7
low-trust 235
open 46, 47
primordial 235, 237
rigid 46, 235
strategic 235–7
strong 46–7
supply chain 235–7
weak 46–7

Newman, Garry 156
Nintendo 79–80, 204
Nissan 121
'No Right Brain Left Behind' 226
Nokia 38, 81, 204
novelty xxvii, 4, 8, 18, 21, 75–6, 79,
99, 109, 235
fetish 29
outliers 7
Nunes, Paul F. 219
nurturing (of ideas) 5, 16, 85

objectives xix, 37
Obokata, Haruko 187
O'Neil, Jack 133
O'Neil, Pat 133
Ono, Yoko 65
OODA loop 132, 239, 241
opportunity 11–12, 22, 27, 29, 49,
62, 79, 82, 92, 99–100, 102,
123–4, 131–2, 144–5, 153, 183,
187, 197, 214, 227
order xxvii–xxviii, 6, 185 see also
convergence
organisation
of people 43–5, 47–8, 131
organisations 39–40, 46, 49, 52,
54–5, 92, 121, 197, 223–5, 228,
233
ambidextrous 45–6
bottom up 36–7, 55
culture of see culture
mechanistic 45
organic 45–6
structure of 48
top down 36, 38, 45, 47, 55
orienting 240
Osborn, Alex xxiv, 158
Applied Imagination 158
Osterwalder, Alex 165
outsourcing 224–5, 235

An elusive moment when a new
idea strikes that has the potential to
transform the way you do business

ISBN: 9781292005287 | eBook: 9781292005317

The Spark

Greg Orme

"Insightful, inspiring and practical. *The Spark* is essential reading
for anyone wanting to harness creativity to drive business success."
Wil Harris, Head of Digital, Condé Nast UK

The
Spark

How to Ignite and Lead
Business Creativity

Greg Orme

FT PUBLISHING
FINANCIAL TIMES

"Greg Orme has put
his finger on the pulse
of creative businesses
and come up with a
remarkable handbook
for founders, managers
and employees trying
to create or recreate
the type of environment
they need to grow and
succeed - bravo!"

John Bates, Fellow in Strategy
& Entrepreneurship at
London Business School

The Spark unravels the mystique around business creativity
and offers 10 practical steps to build an innovative team and
become an inspiring creative leader.

 FTPublishing   @FTPH

 FT PUBLISHING
FINANCIAL TIMES